THE ONE MINUTE
WINE MASTER

THE ONE MINUTE WINE MASTER

DISCOVER 10 WINES YOU'LL LIKE IN 60 SECONDS OR LESS

JENNIFER SIMONETTI-BRYAN, MW

STERLING EPICURE
New York

STERLING EPICURE
New York

An Imprint of Sterling Publishing
387 Park Avenue South
New York, NY 10016

© 2012 by Jennifer Simonetti-Bryan

Illustrations by Peter Hoey

ISBN 978-1-4027-8022-6

Distributed in Canada by Sterling Publishing
c/o Canadian Manda Group, 165 Dufferin Street
Toronto, Ontario, Canada M6K 3H6
Distributed in the United Kingdom by GMC Distribution Services
Castle Place, 166 High Street, Lewes, East Sussex, England BN7 1XU
Distributed in Australia by Capricorn Link (Australia) Pty. Ltd.
P.O. Box 704, Windsor, NSW 2756, Australia

For information about custom editions, special sales, and premium and
corporate purchases, please contact Sterling Special Sales at 800-805-5489
or specialsales@sterlingpublishing.com.

Printed in China

2   4   6   8   10   9   7   5   3

www.sterlingpublishing.com

*This book is dedicated to all of those who long
to follow their passions (or to find a new one).
You are closer than you think.*

*May all your joys be pure joys and
all your pain champagne!*

CONTENTS

INTRODUCTION

WHERE DID YOUR LOVE FOR WINE BEGIN?

I love hearing how people's interest in wine was born. For me, it was a business lunch that changed my life—forever.

I was working for Citibank in London as a management associate and one day we had a lunch meeting in our executive dining room. In the U.S. corporate world, there are three beverage choices—water, iced tea, and soda of some sort. When I was in banking in New York, it was frowned upon to have alcohol of any kind at lunch.

However, because we were in London, and it was a client presentation, wine was part of the meal. I was excited as I knew nothing about wine and it sparked my curiosity.

Lunch was herb-crusted salmon served with a chilled glass of Sancerre. I know now that Sancerre is a white wine from the Loire Valley in France. Salmon is a very fatty fish. The next time you take a bite of salmon, notice how it coats your tongue with oil. Sancerre is made from an acidic grape variety called Sauvignon Blanc.

When I followed a bite of the salmon with a sip of the Sancerre, I noticed the wine created a refreshing sensation in my mouth. It was as if the wine were cleansing the oil from my tongue, preparing me for that next delicious bite. Simultaneously, the flavor of the herbs on the salmon helped my palate focus on the wine's fruitiness, making it taste like fresh, ripe lemons and limes, and the acidity made all the flavors come alive in my mouth.

I'd never experienced anything like this before. I was absolutely blown away. Actually, I couldn't pay attention at the meeting as I kept interrupting people to say, "Try the salmon . . . and *now* try the wine!"

From that moment on, my eyes were opened to an entire new world of aromas, flavors, textures—a heightened awareness of these senses and sensations.

However, I came to realize that not everyone appreciates wine in exactly the same way I do. Though the client at the lunch meeting shared my food and wine–pairing epiphany, I was ridiculed by my colleagues for being distracted.

INSPIRATION FOR THE BOOK

You probably assume that because I've achieved the Master of Wine title, I must have grown up sipping from my father's two-thousand-bottle cellar. Nothing could be further from the truth. In fact, my family doesn't really drink. Don't get me wrong, they have nothing against it. It's just that it was never a big part of our family functions or parties.

Shortly after I left banking, I visited my family with a bottle of wine. This was a wine I thought was stellar. I couldn't wait to share it with them and to hear their exclamations: *"Wow!"* or *"I've never tasted a wine like this!"* or *"It's amazing!"*

The wine I brought home on that occasion was a 1996 Grands Échezeaux—a grand cru Burgundy and one very expensive wine. My family had never spent more than $10 for a bottle of wine, and I wanted to show them how beautiful wine could be—an almost ethereal, sensual experience.

So, I opened the wine, tasted it, reveled in its complexity. I started to talk about how it was made, where it was from, and where Burgundy is on the map. Then I left the room for a minute. When I came back, my family had added 7 Up to their glasses! They had made a $200 spritzer! They said the wine tasted too sour and it needed some sugar. I was floored.

Even my identical twin sister didn't like it! Here was the one person in the world I thought would understand me and my amazing wine. After all, I loved it and we are genetically identical. But she didn't. This taught me that no two people have the same palate, no matter how similar they are.

On a separate occasion, my mom told me she had bought some wine for a party with some friends and that she didn't like it very much. I asked her what she had bought and she said, "Oh, I don't know. It's got a pretty label, though, and I was so disappointed. What should I buy next time?"

I was so excited to impart some of my newfound wine knowledge to her. I started to explain my philosophies on how to buy wines, taste differences between the top "noble grape" varieties, where they are grown, how the soil and climate impact the flavor, books she should read, and so on and so on.

But after a few minutes I noticed her eyes start to glaze over, and she gave me this "That's nice, honey" kind of look. I realized that she didn't want my wine knowledge. She didn't want to read about wine, she didn't want to do any research or look up ratings or memorize anything. She just wanted me to tell her what she would like and give her a few examples.

From these situations and others like it, I learned that the range of wine preferences is wide and any answer to "What kind of wine do you think I would like?" should be short, quick, and to the point.

The One Minute Wine Master does this and it does it faster than any other wine book ever has.

HOW TO USE THIS BOOK

Of course I hope you'll read all of the chapters leading up to *The One Minute Wine Master* Quiz and everything that comes after, and that you won't skip to just the parts that apply directly to you and your palate.

But if the suspense is killing you, skip to chapter 5. Take *The One Minute Wine Master* Quiz and read the season that corresponds to your answers (or just go straight to the wheel and cheat sheet, also in chapter 5). I won't tell. However, to get the most out of this book, come back to the chapters you've skipped to understand why the quiz works (or why it doesn't work perfectly for you). These chapters will help you get the most out of your wine experience.

1

WHO IS THE ONE MINUTE WINE MASTER?

THE ONE MINUTE WINE MASTER IS YOU. IT'S ME. It's your family, your friends, your clients, your coworkers, your spouse, your girlfriend or boyfriend. We are all One Minute Wine Masters. This book is for all of us. This book will help you figure out your individual preferences so that you can find wines you will like again and again (and in less than one minute).

When people say to me "I don't like wine," I reply, "You just haven't found the right one!" The beauty of wine is that its aromas, flavors, and textures are so diverse that there is a wine out there for everyone, one that you will like (and likely more than just one).

I've personally met thousands of wine drinkers all over the world. The one thing we have in common is that we all like wine. Quite possibly, though, that may be the only thing we have in common. Some people know what they like, some don't have a clue, and others like anything you put in their glass.

I love wine because it is a personal, individual experience. My experience with wine is unique to me. No two people experience wine the same way.

Before we get there, let's meet a few wine drinkers and see if any of them sound like you or people you know.

MICHELLE— THE "OVERWHELMED" WINE DRINKER

I do all the shopping—food shopping, clothes shopping, and even wine shopping. I buy wine for family functions and for get-togethers with our friends. I wish I knew more because every time I walk into the store, it's just dizzying to deal with the number of wines that are in the aisle. I can't read half the stuff on the label nor do I want to. I just want something good, you know? And you can never find anyone who can help you.

One time I heard these two women talking about wine in the aisle just a little ways from me and they were saying stuff like, "Oh yes, I get lots of typical varietal flavors like gooseberry and fresh-cut grass," and "I hate all the oaky flavor in that Chardonnay." What's all that mean anyway? Isn't this supposed to be wine? Just drink the stuff!

Most of the time, I get so frustrated I just end up buying the prettiest bottle (or whatever is on sale) because it's all the same to me. Sometimes I don't buy anything at all because I don't want to waste my money buying the wrong thing.

Michelle is what we in the industry call an Overwhelmed consumer. These shoppers get anxious when confronted with the sheer volume and assortment of wines on store shelves. I don't blame them. Some wine stores carry more than three thousand different wines.

There are hundreds of thousands of wines in the world, and new brands are produced every year. More than 3,300 new wine brands were launched in U.S. grocery stores from 1999 to 2007 alone. That's a lot!

> *Some wine stores carry more than three thousand different wines.*
>
> **"**

Think about it this way: Perdue is a brand name of chicken products. Now imagine if you had over three thousand new brand names of chicken to choose from at the supermarket. If you are like Michelle (the Overwhelmed wine drinker) you might become so frustrated that you suddenly devote your life to vegetarianism.

These Overwhelmed drinkers like wine, but don't know what kind to buy and generally choose a wine while feeling under pressure. They are open to advice, but want easy-to-understand information on the label.

If this is you, don't worry: you are not alone. A 2007 industry study commissioned by Constellation Wines called Project Genome found that 23 percent of all wine drinkers are in this boat. There are literally millions of you. This book will help you feel less overwhelmed and more empowered to make better wine selections.

CAROLINE— THE "SATISFIED SIPPER"

I don't know much about wine, but I know what I like to drink. I usually buy the same bottle over and over because it's my tried and true. I know I like it, so I'm not wasting my money. It also saves me time when shopping. I run in, get what I want, and run out.

I hate the snobby airs people put on about wine, so I don't stay very long in the wine aisle or wine store. Who has time to read back labels or strike up a conversation with anyone in the store? It's just wine, not rocket science! I am totally happy with my wine. And if I can buy a bigger bottle of my wine, that's even better. It lasts longer!

Caroline is what the industry calls a Satisfied Sipper. My grandmother (whose name also happens to be Caroline) is a Satisfied Sipper. This category makes up 14 percent of wine drinkers. They generally buy one brand (with my family it was Riunite) and stick with it. They are completely satisfied if that's the only wine they ever have.

Satisfied Sippers are not very open to buying new wines for fear of making a mistake or wasting their money on something they won't like. They hate the whole wine-buying process. Their eyes also glaze over if someone starts talking about how the wine is made or where it comes from. They're not very interested in that sort of thing.

If this sounds like you, this book will help you choose wines you like in less time, without having to read labels, talk with staff, or do any background homework.

Project Genome estimated that 37 percent of all wine drinkers feel like either Michelle or Caroline. If that doesn't sound like a lot, consider this—back in 2009, *Food & Wine* magazine estimated that the number of wine drinkers would increase to about 148 million people within the next three years. If that's true, these two categories alone would make up approximately 55 million people. That's more than the entire population of England and double the population of Australia!

> **They generally buy one brand and stick with it.**

BOB—THE "TRADITIONALIST"

I do enjoy wine and I drink wine. Can't say that I'm an expert and I don't have a cellar or anything, but I know the ones I like. It's not an everyday thing. To be honest, I really drink wine just on special occasions.

Sometimes I get to try new wines at these events because they have nothing else, but for the most part I stick to my favorites.

Traditionalists represent about 16 percent of wine drinkers. They enjoy wine, but generally save it for more formal occasions with family and friends.

Traditionalists care a bit more about wine brand names than those in the Overwhelmed and Satisfied Sipper categories. They like a wide variety of well-known brands because they feel established brand names point to reliability and quality. However, just like the Overwhelmed and Satisfied Sippers, they are often too intimidated to try new wines. If you're a Traditionalist, this book will help you feel less intimidated and help you choose wines that suit your individual palate perfectly.

> *They enjoy wine, but generally save it for more formal occasions.*

When you add up these three categories—Overwhelmed, Satisfied Sippers, and Traditionalists—over half of the wine drinkers, possibly soon more than seventy-eight million Americans, are intimidated to try new wines.

JIM—THE WINE "ENTHUSIAST"

I drink wine often and I consider myself somewhat knowledgeable. I like reading up on wine, reading wine magazines and wine blogs. And I like going to wine tastings, especially up at my wine store because it gives me the chance to taste before I buy. I entertain at home a lot with friends and we often have wine parties where we pair foods with different wines.

I like knowing where in the world my wine came from, the types of grapes it's made from, etc. There's a sense of adventure with it. I take my Chianti Classico, point to the region on a map in Italy, and whenever I taste it I feel transported to Italy. I try to imagine the Tuscan sun on my face, and walking along ancient cobblestone roads and smelling the fresh oregano in the air.

> **Enthusiasts love to browse the wine section.**

Jim is what is considered an Enthusiast by the Project Genome study. Enthusiasts love to browse the wine section and read wine publications, and are influenced by wine critics, ratings, and reviews. For you Enthusiasts, *The One Minute Wine Master* will help you select new wines to explore for you and your friends.

Despite Enthusiasts' enormous excitement and passion for wine, they are actually the smallest group, making up only 12 percent of wine drinkers.

BILL—THE "IMAGE SEEKER"

I do a lot of client entertaining. I meet clients for drinks or dinner, and wine is a large part of that. Before going to a restaurant with clients, I check out the wine list online and see what the critics say about it. I want to make sure there are recognized top-tier wines. I enjoy the research, but more than that, I don't want to be embarrassed in front of clients, and this is a great way for me to stand out and impress them.

Bill would be identified by Project Genome as an Image Seeker. Image Seekers feel they have a basic knowledge of wine and are excited to explore new ones. However, what makes Image Seekers different from Enthusiasts is that they view wine as a tool to demonstrate status.

Anyone who has ever entertained clients knows the scene: You and your colleagues are at "Chez Fancy," nervously making conversation with Mr. Big Client and his team. Fancy Sommelier comes to the table with a wine list that looks thicker than the Bible and drops it on the table with a loud *whap*!

Now comes my favorite part. The wine list is suddenly a very hot potato. Each person tosses it to his or her right or left saying, "Uh . . . you choose the wine."

Picking the restaurant for a client dinner is hard enough. But when choosing wine, there is a real fear of making the wrong choice and looking unsophisticated or foolish.

But in my experience, if one person takes charge, grabs the wine list, and makes a decision on the wine, he/she earns a bit of extra respect. It doesn't seem to matter what the wine is or if everyone actually enjoys it. The chooser gets kudos just for making the choice. And if you manage to pick something Mr. Big Client likes, you become the superstar for the evening.

Image Seekers may not be trying to impress only clients. It may be that "special someone" on a date. The point is they see wine as something that can help them look good.

The term "Image Seeker" may bring to mind a group that is snobby and elitist. I don't believe that's the case. These wine drinkers are pragmatists and understand that wine can be enjoyed and used to their benefit.

Wine is still a delicious beverage to Image Seekers, but that's not all: it makes them feel more important, special, and is a way to potentially advance a relationship. And before you judge this group by their title, know that they make up 20 percent of wine drinkers. So there are millions of them out there as well!

For you Image Seekers, this book will help you choose wines for any occasion, from client dinners to family functions. It will also enhance your ability to use wine as a conversation starter that will help you impress!

JANE—THE "SAVVY SHOPPER"

My husband and I, we know wine. I get the catalogues and e-mails from some wine stores in the city and I see which stores have high margins and know when the best wines are up for discount soon. We already love wine, but those gems (those great wines for a value price) taste that much better!

> **Savvy Shoppers love the wine-shopping experience.**

Another group in the study, called Savvy Shoppers, makes up about 15 percent of wine drinkers. They are similar to Enthusiasts because they are not afraid to explore wines made from unfamiliar grape varieties, new styles and wine regions, etc. Savvy Shoppers love the wine-shopping experience.

What makes them different from Enthusiasts is their love of the bargain. This doesn't mean they buy cheap wine. They are interested in value for money at all price points and get a jolt of excitement from finding the best deal. They have no problem going to different stores or Web sites to get the best deal on a particular wine. Savvy Shoppers also have a few favorites at home as a backup to supplement any disappointing explorations. If you are an Enthusiast, this book will help you make better selections and provide strategies to help you get the best deal.

SO WHO ARE YOU?

You may find that you fit one category very easily. Perhaps you have things in common with more than one category of wine drinker and are more of a blend. That's OK. I'm not trying to put you in a box. That's the last thing I would ever do. I hope this book expands horizons rather than limits them.

I point out these types of wine drinkers to show that there are millions of people just like you, possibly thinking in a similar way. It's also to show you others who have different perspectives on wine.

These categories also teach us a few things. First, almost all wine drinkers want to feel less intimidated by wine. Second, they want to drink the best wine for their lifestyle, their palate, their own experience.

CATEGORIES OF WINE DRINKERS

2007 CONSTELLATION WINE PROJECT GENOME STUDY

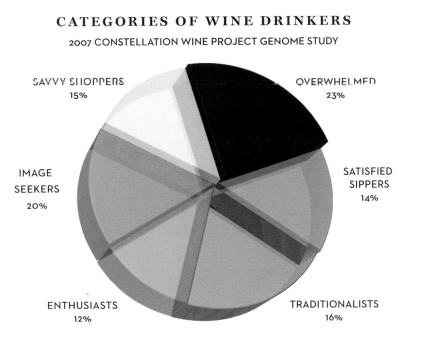

SAVVY SHOPPERS
15%

OVERWHELMED
23%

IMAGE
SEEKERS
20%

SATISFIED
SIPPERS
14%

ENTHUSIASTS
12%

TRADITIONALISTS
16%

Source: "Many Wine Consumers 'Overwhelmed'," *Wines & Vines*, March 10, 2008

The truth of the matter is that there are too many wines out there to think about, let alone commit to memory. With four thousand wine-grape varieties, twenty million acres of vineyards, and many thousands of wineries throughout the world, each with its own unique stamp and every vintage tasting different, the combinations are endless. I'm a Master of Wine and it is hard for me to keep up with it all!

Most wine guides mean well, but they end up giving us even more to memorize—108 shortcuts, one hundred wines under $15, tens of thousands of ratings and tasting notes. One annual guide even boasts over fifty thousand reviews!

In this age of multitasking, texting, and 140-character tweets, we have neither the time nor the patience to read through thousands of reviews or to memorize anything. I created *The One Minute Wine Master* system to simplify it all in less than one minute.

SO HOW DOES
THE ONE MINUTE WINE MASTER WORK?

On page 52, you will see *The One Minute Wine Master* Quiz. The quiz is a set of multiple-choice questions designed to help identify your wine preferences.

Don't know anything about wine? That's OK! These are questions anyone can answer, and fast. There are only eleven simple questions, so it should take you under a minute to complete.

Don't be surprised, though, that the questions are not directly about wine. Each one helps to understand your palate's preferences.

Each answer choice has a particular number of points associated with it. At the end, after you have answered each question, you will need to tally up your total points.

Your score will place you into one of four seasonal categories—Spring, Summer, Fall, or Winter. Each season has its own set of characteristics. It's a concept similar to that of zodiac signs, for which some believe those born within the same signs or moon phases share similar personality traits. *The One Minute Wine Master* doesn't reveal personality traits, but it will point to wines you are likely to enjoy based on your quiz answers.

Right now, you may be asking yourself, "Will this really work for me?"

Yes. It will in whole or in part. Like anything in life, you get the most out of it when you understand why.

Your quiz results may be more complex than you think, and these earlier chapters will help simplify things. By reading the chapters leading up to the quiz, you will understand yourself and your personal preferences better.

KNOW THYSELF

"We have all a better guide in ourselves, if we would attend to it, than any other person can be."

—JANE AUSTEN

YOU'VE JUST DISCOVERED YOU ARE A ONE MINUTE WINE MASTER. "OK. So now what?" you may be thinking.

In order to make better wine choices for yourself and others, your next step is to explore why you have certain preferences. You need to know about you.

In this chapter we will get a better understanding of your palate and what makes you like the types of wines that you do. In other words, you will learn what makes you tick (in terms of wine, anyway).

First, let's take a look at what your mind is telling you and what your biases (if any) might be. Don't think you have taste biases? Neither did I.

TERRIBLE CRAB CAKES

I attended my first conference dinner while I was in college. Coming from somewhat humble beginnings, I was dazzled by the banquet hall, the fancy tablecloths, and beautiful china. I felt so important just being there.

The formally uniformed waiters came out and served the first course. I recognized it immediately—crab cakes, one of my favorites!

I excitedly took my first bite and I knew something was wrong. This crab cake tasted terrible. I was immediately concerned that everyone at my table would get sick. After all, this was fish we were talking about! So I anxiously called a waiter over and explained that there was something wrong with the crab cake.

After several minutes, I saw all the other tables happily eating their crab cakes, not knowing the dangers that were about to befall them! In a panic, I got up from the table to find a manager and told him people would get sick from the crab cakes if he didn't do something fast.

But he laughed at me! Before I got really mad, he whispered, "Miss, there is nothing wrong with your dish. It's a corn cake, not a crab cake."

Oh! I tasted the dish again. He was right. He was right, and in fact it was a very good corn cake. Terrible crab cake, but great corn cake!

This embarrassing situation taught me the very valuable lesson that my expectations and biases have an enormous impact on my perception of taste.

Do you have any preconceived notions or expectations about wines? These expectations might be helping you identify wines you like, but also be aware that they may be getting in the way of enjoying something even more delicious.

Where do these biases come from? Mostly they come from stereotypes and word of mouth, but there is also something I call First Love Syndrome.

STEREOTYPES

Wine has not escaped the many stereotypes in our society. One I've heard is that men are supposed to want big, rich, tannic, full-bodied, macho red wines while women are supposed to like delicate, floral, fresh white wines.

I have met many men who do a ton of client entertaining who sound almost apologetic when they say, "I know I'm supposed to like the California Cabs or Bordeaux wines. I entertain with them all the time because they're expensive and everyone loves them, but they're not my style."

I've also had women say to me, "All of my friends drink White Zinfandel and Pinot Grigio, but I really love red wine. Am I weird?"

Let me tell you straight. There is nothing wrong with you or your palate. In fact, this is probably a really good time to say that there is no right and wrong with wine. There is only what you like and don't like. At the end of this process you will find out what your preferences are—they are individual to you. And there is nothing wrong with that!

WORD OF MOUTH

Many marketing studies suggest that word of mouth is the number one factor influencing our decisions to purchase something specific. It's pretty powerful stuff.

We love recommendations especially when they come from people we think know what they are talking about. This could be your best friend or your boss, or maybe you read blogs or reviews by acclaimed critics. There are so many wines out there that this can be a great way to identify new wines to try.

However, the problem with taking a recommendation, whether for a movie or a bottle of wine, is that it is based on someone else's opinion. Now, I don't know about you, but I don't always share the same tastes in wines (or movies) as my friends, family, and coworkers.

Does that mean you shouldn't buy a wine based on a good recommendation? No. A recommendation from someone can be extremely useful, particularly if you have similar palates. In chapter 12, I'll teach you my secret to identifying which critics to follow for your individual palate.

THE "FIRST LOVE" SYNDROME

As I was writing this book, I was on the *Today* show to talk about my wine personality quiz (the beginnings of *The One Minute Wine Master* taking form). I had asked the show's hosts, Kathie Lee Gifford and Hoda Kotb, to take in advance a quiz that is now *The One Minute Wine Master* Quiz. Kathie Lee's results indicated that she was barely over the threshold from Spring into Summer. She was a cusp Spring. (This will make sense after you read chapter 5.)

In the quiz, her answers indicated she likes light-bodied white wines, has a high tolerance for acidity, and prefers fresh and floral scents.

Based on this, I might have recommended she try a Sauvignon Blanc—a Spring variety that you will see in chapter 7. But weeks earlier I had seen her on a show where she said she hates Sauvignon Blanc. So I recommended a Spring-Summer cusp wine, like a Pinot Noir, but she said, "No, not really." I began to suspect she might be a closet Fall because she frequently speaks of her love for California Chardonnays on the show. However, based on her quiz answers, she wouldn't like this wine.

So why did she have eyes only for a full-bodied, buttery California Chardonnay (a Fall wine) despite her quiz answers and all indications to the contrary? It could be that my questions at the time were too vague (I've since changed them). Or it could be what I call (in wine) the First Love Syndrome. We fall in love with a wine. Perhaps it was the wine you first had with your sweetheart, or maybe it was a wine you had on a vacation, or it is the favorite of someone you really look up to. Every sip takes you back to that wonderful time or reminds you of that fabulous person. This is biological. Studies have shown a powerful connection between aromas/flavors and memory.

But whatever the reason, you and this wine found each other and that's it. You are smitten and you have a history together. Some even categorize themselves as "Chardonnay drinkers" or "Merlot drinkers" or "Chianti drinkers." They have identified themselves with that particular wine.

I can understand why this happens. Given the variety of available wines, once you find one you like, things get simpler. You then have your choice wine! It may also be because you just got used to it and it's easy. You don't think you have to look much further.

In elementary school I drank whole milk at lunch every day. That is, until one day the school switched to skim milk. I hated skim milk, but I drank it every day anyway. Then, after a few weeks, they offered whole milk again, and I found something interesting. I had gotten used to the skim milk and I no longer liked the whole milk! This was an early lesson for me that one can get used to a particular taste, and that tastes can change. It can be the same with wine. You may have had your "favorite" wine for so long that you cannot see anything else.

Actually, having a particular favorite wine is not a bad thing, far from it. At least you know what you like. However, be aware that you may have blinders on to other wines. You could be missing out on some incredible taste experiences!

I say this because you may take a look at your results from the quiz and think, "That's not me! I don't like those wines." Keep an open mind and try a few that you might never have tasted before. It may be a good idea to invite some friends over so you don't have to worry about wasting an entire bottle if you don't like it.

Is it guaranteed you will like all the wines in your category? Of course not. There are so many factors that go into the equation. Let me use art as an analogy. Let's look at the artists Picasso (from his black and blue periods) and Monet. Both Picasso and Monet used the color blue in their paintings, but these artists could not be more different in their artistic expressions. So if you say you like blue, can I say you will prefer Picasso to Monet? More information is needed. That's why it's important to understand the reasoning behind the questions so that you can target your individual palate.

So keep an open mind and expand your palate's horizons. You may be surprised and find some new favorites.

MYTH—"I'M JUST NOT THAT GOOD AT TASTING WINE"

I cannot tell you how many times I have heard people say this—from people who have never picked up a glass before to wine professionals. It's rubbish! There is no reason to be insecure about your tasting abilities.

Sure there are people who know more about wine than you. They may have developed their education and palate more than you at this point. However, your palate is unique. No one can be a better you than you or know better what you like. So trust your palate.

Two years ago, I was listening to a tasting presentation on Cognac. I know Cognac is not wine, but bear with me. We all tasted through the different Cognacs and the presenter asked, "What aromas did you get in the first glass?" One gentleman raised his hand and answered that he smelled "apricot pastry or Danish." The presenter then proceeded to embarrass the gentleman by saying, "No. That is not what you taste."

I was so offended on this gentleman's behalf! First, it takes courage to be the first to say something. How dare this presenter tell someone that is not what he tasted! Is the presenter inside this gentleman's nose? No. Is the presenter tasting with this gentleman's taste buds? Of course not! Only you know what you are smelling and tasting. Sure, there are general tendencies (Chardonnay tastes of apples, Riesling is a high-acid grape, etc.), but there is no "wrong" in exploring and vocalizing what your nose and taste buds are telling you.

Whether you are reading this book just to pick out a few new favorites or you want to jump-start your newfound passion for wine, don't feel intimidated into thinking you do not have a "great palate." This is the fun part! I'm a Master of Wine and I won an international trophy for my palate. However, I try to improve my palate and tasting skills every day. It's a journey, it's not a destination. And the great thing about wanting to learn how to taste wine is that it involves tasting more wine!

Now that you are aware of your biases and how your mind influences what you like, let's look into what your body is actually telling you.

AROMAS, FLAVORS, AND TASTE

THE NOSE KNOWS

OUR SENSE OF SMELL IS IMPORTANT. When there's a fire, it can alert us far in advance of seeing flames or feeling heat. When food is spoiled, we recoil because it smells rotten and we don't eat it, saving us from sickness. Some scientists even talk of the relationship between the sense of smell and choosing a mate. (My sister still makes fun of me for dumping a perfectly handsome and successful guy because he always smelled like bad chicken soup to me.)

Your sense of smell is one of the most important tools when tasting wine. Why? Because what you think you perceive as flavors are actually aromas.

When you smell wine, aromatic compounds travel up your nose and reach chemical receptor cells high up in your nasal cavity. The receptors send signals to the olfactory bulb, which tells your brain what you smell.

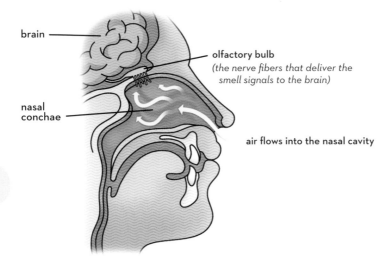

brain

olfactory bulb
*(the nerve fibers that deliver the
smell signals to the brain)*

nasal
conchae

air flows into the nasal cavity

You can also smell flavors after you've swallowed something. However, after you have swallowed wine, the aromas don't travel through your nose, but behind your tongue, and then up through your retronasal cavity to those receptors. (Not to be crude, but this also explains why after burping you can sometimes taste things you have eaten hours earlier.)

Think of any food or beverage that you love—coffee, chocolate, ice cream, popcorn, burgers, cheesecake, cinnamon rolls, etc. What you think are flavors are actually aromas.

Don't believe me? Remember what it was like the last time you had a cold or bad allergy? You couldn't breathe through your nose because it was so stuffy, and you couldn't taste anything. When you have a cold or bad allergy, your nasal passages become congested. This blocks the path of those aromatic compounds to the receptors, preventing you from perceiving any scent, aroma, or flavor whatsoever.

Scientists have also shown that our sense of smell, more than any other sense, is intimately connected to emotion. We receive stimuli in the olfactory bulb and then translate the stimuli into perception. However, the olfactory bulb is part of the limbic system, which also includes the amygdala and hippocampus, both linked to our behavior, mood, and memory. This is why certain smells conjure up powerful memories.

One day on the streets of Manhattan I must have walked by someone who wore the same perfume as my late grandmother. I was immediately transported to her home, sitting at her kitchen table, watching her cook. It was like she was there. Ever have an experience like that? Our sense of smell is linked to memories. It's quite powerful.

Some people are very sensitive to smell in general and some are very sensitive to specific aromas. For example, I am very sensitive to a chemical found in wine called methoxypyrazine. (You don't have to memorize this, don't worry.) Methoxypyrazine is a chemical responsible for the aromas found in green bell peppers. It's also found in some Cabernet Sauvignons. I'm not sure if I'm allergic to it, or if I just don't like it, but my nose is sensitive to it. It helped me on my Master of Wine exam. If a wine has a little Cabernet Sauvignon in the blend, I can detect it.

Sure, I fine-tuned my sense of smell over the better part of a decade in preparation for the exam. However, I don't get some aromas that some people swear they identify in wine. For example, I have fellow MWs who have said that Grüner Veltliner, a white wine originally from Austria, clearly smells of lentils. To be honest, it never smelled like lentils to me. Does that mean I'm deficient in some way? Does that mean my palate's bad? No. It just means I don't smell lentils in Grüner Veltliner. And that's OK.

However, there are some unfortunate people who have a condition called anosmia. Anosmia is the inability to perceive odors. Similar to color blindness, some people cannot perceive a specific scent. This is called a specific anosmia, or the inability to smell a particular aromatic compound. This may explain why I can never perceive the compound responsible for the aroma of lentils in wine.

Most people, however, when they are starting out in wine, do not perceive aromas/flavors in wine because they have problems identifying what their palate is telling them. I have had numerous students say, "Jennifer, what is that I'm smelling in this wine?" I could only reply with, "I don't know. What is your nose telling you? What does it smell like to you?"

The reality is that we do not practice our sense of smell the way we practice sight or touch. Allow me to use an analogy with a box of crayons. When we were small, we get our first box of crayons with eight colors in it (red, orange, yellow, green, blue, purple, brown, black). We are content coloring in our coloring books, but then we get the sixteen-crayon box, and then the thirty-two-crayon box that not only has red and orange, but also a crayon called red-orange that is different from orange-red. Next is the mother lode of all crayon boxes—the box of sixty-four. This has blue and green crayons, but also teal blue, turquoise blue, aquamarine, and periwinkle. Each has its own distinctive color.

If I asked you to tell me the difference between teal blue and turquoise blue, many of you would be able to do it with no problem. It's because you practiced knowing your colors starting with crayons. Inadvertently, possibly, but you still practiced. And the same thing goes for your sense of smell. You can practice and get better at it.

HOW DO I IMPROVE MY SENSE OF SMELL?

The cheapest way to improve your sense of smell is to simply take more notice of aromas all around you. Make a mental note of different aromas and flavors when you eat. That's a good start!

You can also go to your kitchen cabinet or spice rack and take some things out—cinnamon, nutmeg, coriander, dried cherries, walnuts, for example. It can be a fun exercise to go to the supermarket and pick up some items that are typically found in wine—lemons, limes, passion fruit, peaches, nectarines, apricots, cherries (red and black), raspberries, blackberries, and so on. Cut into them, smell them, taste them, and register how each tastes. You may also want to smell all of the individual herbs in the spices aisle in the supermarket.

Ann Noble at the University of California at Davis came out with a Wine Aroma Wheel to help people identify aromas. This wheel is very good when you are a bit more advanced. However, when I first started getting into wine and I took a look at this wheel, it intimidated me. There were way too many things on it for me to process. It's quite comprehensive, so it includes more advanced aromas and unpleasant aromas for identifying faults one can find in wine.

Sticking with my crayon analogy, below is the box of eight with some sample descriptions you can start with:

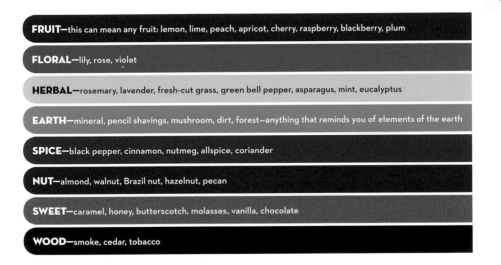

FRUIT—this can mean any fruit: lemon, lime, peach, apricot, cherry, raspberry, blackberry, plum

FLORAL—lily, rose, violet

HERBAL—rosemary, lavender, fresh-cut grass, green bell pepper, asparagus, mint, eucalyptus

EARTH—mineral, pencil shavings, mushroom, dirt, forest—anything that reminds you of elements of the earth

SPICE—black pepper, cinnamon, nutmeg, allspice, coriander

NUT—almond, walnut, Brazil nut, hazelnut, pecan

SWEET—caramel, honey, butterscotch, molasses, vanilla, chocolate

WOOD—smoke, cedar, tobacco

Will wine taste exactly like these things? Yes and no. When we say "This tastes just like chocolate-covered cherries" or "I get lemon flavors," it means that something reminiscent of those aromas and flavors registers in our brains. It doesn't necessarily mean it's going to be exactly like that.

You may think only "fruit" when you smell wine and not be able to dig any deeper for a description. That's OK! With time and practice, just like with the crayons when you were young, you will be able to see from blue and green to the finer shades of aquamarine and teal blue. It didn't happen overnight for me, and I'm still learning and fine-tuning.

One way I improved my sense of smell was with the Le Nez du Vin (or "The Nose of Wine" in French) set. It's a wine aroma kit—a collection of tiny bottles of aromas in essential oils and other liquids. I started with the kit with twenty-four aromas in it.

The bottles are numbered and come with a brochure that has the numbers and corresponding aromas. I would take one bottle, say number fifteen—cherry—and really sit there smelling it, registering it, and knowing it as cherry. Then, after a while, I would take the bottles out of the box, hide the brochure so I wouldn't know what was in which tiny bottle, and test myself. I would see if I could identify an aroma blind (meaning I would pick up a random aroma while my eyes were closed so I couldn't cheat to see what it was). Then I would take two tiny bottles together and smell them at the same time to see if I could separate out and identify cherry and walnut, or honey and butter. This took a long time, and there are still some aromas I have to peek at the brochure to be sure of.

Why should you care about smelling different things in wine? Again, aromas are flavors. Understanding the flavors you perceive adds to your connection with the wine and enhances your experience with it.

WHAT'S YOUR TONGUE TELLING YOU?

Try this test. Close your nose and eat a piece of chocolate. See how much flavor you are getting. Not much, right? When you take your hand away from your nose, while still having some chocolate left in your mouth, you get a huge rush of flavor as you breathe in through your nose. Your tongue can't perceive flavor (remember, when you have a cold you can't smell anything and food seems to be flavorless). It's your nose that helps you perceive flavor. As we mentioned before, flavors are actually aromas. So what is it your tongue tastes?

While there are approximately two hundred compounds the human nose can perceive in wine, your tongue can perceive texture, temperature, and five tastes—sweet, sour, salty, bitter, and umami.

SWEET

When a wine is sweet, our taste buds tell our brain that it's sweet. Sweetness is easy to perceive, especially for us Americans. We love our sugar. In fact I have heard from many Europeans, "Your food is much sweeter, your drinks are much sweeter, everything you Americans eat and drink is sweet!" That may be true. I know some people would qualify chocolate as its own major food group. A CBS report a few years ago stated the average American consumes 142 pounds of sugar a year, or roughly 3 pounds of sugar a week. We know sweet. Or do we?

The opposite of sweet is dry. One of the biggest mistakes that people make when learning about wine, or about what to ask a sommelier for in a wine, has to do with the definitions of "dry," "sweet," and "fruity." They end up asking for the wrong thing and are often disappointed.

When people say "fruity," that is actually a flavor (and we now know that flavors are aromas). You may want a fruity wine, but that actually has less to do with sweetness than you think. Your tongue can't perceive "fruity." A wine can have a sweet impression of fruit and still be bone dry.

Sweetness, however, is quite different. This is where many people make a mistake and tell the sommelier or the staff at the wine store "I'm looking for a fruity wine" when they are actually looking for a "sweet" wine with a flavor of fruit.

During the Master of Wine exam, I had to identify thirty-six wines blind. One of them, I remember, was a very fruity wine and I thought it might also be slightly sweet. So what did I do? I held my nose and tasted the wine. I knew my tongue would not lie. Turns out it was absolutely bone dry (dry wines are considered anything under 5 grams per liter of residual sugar. This is the average threshold level for humans to perceive sweetness). It was a fruity and a dry wine.

Then there are fruity wines you think are dry, but are not. Take the example of the brand Yellow Tail, from Australia. One of the smartest things they did was to conduct a lot of research and testing with consumers in the United States before creating their brand. What did they find? We like sweet. Therefore the wines they created have a bit more residual sugar in them than technically dry wines. Their wines are very fruity, but some are not technically "dry" (or below 5 grams per liter of residual sugar). The result? Yellow Tail is one of the most successful brands in the United States.

I have noticed that some people will err on the side of saying "I like a dry wine" rather than saying they like a sweet one, even if they prefer wines with a little sweetness. For some reason, we have it in our heads that saying we like a dry wine is more sophisticated than saying we like a sweet one. We have equated sweetness with cheap wines and no one wants to say they prefer cheap wines. But this is not true. Some of the most expensive, longest-lived, and lusciously decadent wines in the world are sweet wines. There is nothing wrong with liking a sweet wine. If you like sweet wines, say it with pride. It's what you like!

You may say to yourself "I don't like anything that has high acidity." Before you make such a judgment, remember that if you like tomato sauce, coffee, yogurt, or corn, you like foods high in acidity.

My Grandma Simonetti must have been less fond of high acidity as she added a special ingredient to her own tomato sauce. I can still remember her talking to my sister and me as she stirred the large sauce pot. She would say, "Now, girls, this is how you do it. Take the sugar and throw in one handful, a second handful and another one for Grandma." That's three handfuls of sugar!

SOUR

Our brains register something as sour when it is high in acidity. Have you ever bitten into a fresh lemon or a sour candy and almost immediately puckered, and the sides of your tongue came alive? That's acidity.

Sounds unpleasant. So why do we care about acidity? Acidity has two main functions in wine: one, it helps us perceive more flavors, and two, it helps the wine age longer.

Acidity is what makes food and beverages refreshing. It stimulates your palate and makes it feel fresh and pure.

Acidity is also important as it can make the aromas/flavors pop. Many people add a dash of lemon juice in cooking because it brings out the flavors more. Sugar, however, actually has the opposite effect. It can mask flavors and aromas. In fact there are some wineries that use sugar as a way to mask some of their wines' faults.

Acidity is much easier to perceive in a wine when it is dry rather than sweet. When wine has sugar you can taste, acidity can be tougher to identify. For example, some German Rieslings may seem low in acid because they are sweet, but they are actually quite high in acidity.

It's the balance between these two that is important. A wine that is not high enough in acid to balance the wine's sweetness is said to be cloying (where the acid isn't enough to cleanse the tongue and the sugar just sits there).

Additionally, acidity can help wines age a great deal longer, especially white wines. While almost all whites are intended to be consumed within three years of the vintage, acidity is the reason some German Rieslings, white Burgundies, and vintage Champagnes can age for decades. These wines last this long because of the excellent balance of the fruit, alcohol, and acidity. However, it's the wine's acidity that is the structural "backbone" of these wines. This is also why some wines made to age can be less pleasant when young, their acidity not having been mellowed by time. For example, some of the best Champagnes from the great 1996 vintage, known for its particularly high acidity, are still considered by some as too young to drink.

Acidity in wine can take some getting used to. Some dry wines may taste sour to you, initially, if you are not used to it. Your palate adapts, however, and after a while the wines likely will not taste as sour. Then you will be able to pick up more of the fruit and other flavors in the wine.

Understand that acidity does have its functions, which help us enjoy flavors more and make our wines last a lot longer.

SALT AND UMAMI

Saltiness is another easy taste for us to sense. Our tongues perceive something as salty when it contains sodium ions. The more sodium ions, the saltier it tastes. There are other alkali metals that contribute to a salty taste, but the further they are from sodium on the periodic table, the less salty they seem.

We do not really taste salt in wine, which makes things easy as we don't have to look for it. However, some wines and fortified wines, such as Muscadet and Fino Sherry, can have a certain aroma reminiscent of brine or salty almonds. These wines are not "salty," but they have aromas that make them almost seem like they are.

Umami takes a little explaining. In Japanese, *umami* translates to "good flavor" or "good taste," though that doesn't help us very much. Many have described it as a "meaty" or "brothy" or "savory" taste, but nothing more concrete than that. This is because there is still some mystery as to how the tongue perceives umami.

Foods that are high in umami are meat, cheese, broth, and other protein-heavy foods. Umami is a taste that is still poorly understood. The important thing for our purposes is that there is no umami in wine.

BITTER/ASTRINGENT

People are generally the most sensitive to bitterness, and you do find bitterness in some wines. Some wines have bitterness because of chemical compounds that we perceive as bitter, such as tannin. Tannin is the primary source of bitterness in wine. Tannin is a chemical that belongs to a compound group called polyphenols (a great word in Scrabble). You may hear wine critics and other people talk interchangeably about tannins and polyphenols, but tannin is a subset of polyphenols. These polyphenols are important.

Tannins in wine come from a few places. They come from the skins, the seeds, the stems, and oak barrels.

Red wines have more bitterness than white wines. Red grapes have white flesh and their juice is white when pressed; the color is extracted from the skins as they sit in the fermenting juice. However, the process is also drawing out tannin and other compounds that can add bitterness. You may perceive tannin in red wine as a gripping or drying sensation in your mouth followed by a bit of bitterness in the aftertaste.

> Have you ever eaten red table grapes (with seeds, meaning not seedless) and chewed on the skin or one of the seeds or accidentally bitten into a stem from a cluster of table grapes? If you haven't, do it intentionally sometime. You will understand that this is where bitterness can come from in the grape.

Like acidity, bitterness can be unpleasant to many, but tannin does have a few functions—it adds texture, it can make a wine last longer, and it may provide some health benefits.

In part because of tannin, red wines have more texture and structure. Wines with a high level of tannin tend to be bolder, with a higher level of fruit—and sometimes alcohol—to balance it out. They tend to be richer, fuller-flavored wines. If not, they are just astringent.

Some white wines have tannin, though never very much. White wines fermented and/or aged in oak, such as many Chardonnays, have more spice flavors (vanilla, nutmeg or other brown spice, toast, etc.) because of the oak, but it also can impart a little bit of bitterness toward the finish. This is not necessarily a bad thing—it can add structure to white wine, just as acidity does, and prolong the wine's life. And white wines can age. Some whites from Burgundy, made from Chardonnay and fermented and aged in oak, are the longest-lived white wines in the world.

As for the health benefits of tannins and polyphenols, have you ever heard that red wine is good for you? Back in 1991, *60 Minutes* aired a program called "The French Paradox" that discussed this very topic. Red wine has polyphenols, which are antioxidants and have been connected with reducing the risk of heart disease. Studies have also linked polyphenols to fighting the common cold, old age, certain types of cancer, obesity, diabetes, and Alzheimer's and other forms of dementia.

But before you think of this as an excuse to drink a lot more wine, think again. Any benefits of wine are associated with moderate consumption. Consumption of alcohol higher than this shows an increased risk of cancer and other health problems. (See Moderate Alcohol Consumption, page 29.)

Bitterness does have its "reasons for being" even if you are not fond of it. Understand, too, that people vary widely in their perception of bitterness.

A wine that tastes terribly bitter to you may taste soft and lusciously fruity to another.

ALCOHOL

My first taste of whiskey was given to me by my uncle at Thanksgiving when I was thirteen. I remember him saying to me, "OK, I'll let you taste it, but let me explain what's going to happen. When you sip it, you are going to feel a sensation like a fire flowing from your mouth down to your toes. It will then rush right up to your head and then fall back down to your toes again." It could have been the power of suggestion on my very impressionable young mind, but he was right! It did taste like a fire that ran all through my system! It was only about a thimbleful, but I will always remember the sensation.

Wines that are particularly high in alcohol seem "hot" on our palate; we feel a sensation like my uncle described. However, we can also taste alcohol as bitterness or as a little sweetness.

Alcohol comes from yeast metabolizing the sugar that's in the grape juice and turning it into alcohol. You might remember from your seventh-grade biology class:

Sugar + Yeast = Alcohol + CO$_2$

The more sugar, the more alcohol is produced. It's as simple as that.

Some grape varieties ripen to higher sugar levels than others, and therefore their wines have a higher alcohol level. Many wines are at about 12 to 13 percent alcohol by volume. Others go quite a bit higher. For example, Grenache (also called Garnacha) is a grape variety found in southern France and Spain. It's a beach bunny. It loves the sun. With all that sun comes a lot of sugar that can be converted into alcohol. Some wines made from Grenache can have alcohol levels of over 15 percent.

However, the same grape variety can vary in sugar depending on where it's grown. Warmer climates generally have grapes that generate more sugar. Take

Chardonnay. It grows in both cool climates and warm climates. Chardonnay grapes grown in Chablis (a very cool region in the north of France) generally lead to an alcohol level of around 12.5 percent. However, Chardonnay grown in the sunny state of California can sometimes get up to 14.5 percent alcohol or more.

MODERATE ALCOHOL CONSUMPTION: WHAT DOES THAT MEAN?

The first time I went to a steak house was in Manhattan. It was for a client dinner when I was still working in corporate banking. We were waiting for our colleagues to arrive so we went to the bar and ordered drinks. I ordered just a glass of white wine. By the time our entire party arrived and it was time for us all to sit down, I had finished my one glass. I got up from the bar to follow my colleagues to the table and . . . oops! I was tipsy! I couldn't figure out why. I had never gotten tipsy on one glass of wine before. So what happened?

The U.S. Department of Health defines one drink as five ounces of wine at about 12 percent alcohol by volume. Moderate consumption is considered one drink per day for women and no more than two drinks per day for men. This can vary widely, however, based on a person's size. The more mass a person has, the less concentrated the alcohol is in their system.

Furthermore, women process alcohol differently than men. Alcohol becomes more concentrated in our bodies because we generally have less muscle mass than men. This is why they can consume more. I know it sounds unfair. However, studies have shown that women have a more developed sense of smell. I guess in some ways it balances out.

So why was I tipsy from one glass of wine? The answer is simple—the size of the glass. I've gone back to that steak house and they pour approximately eight-ounce servings. That is more than 1.5 times the daily allowance for women and almost the daily allowance for men.

Glasses are bigger at some restaurants. Why? Larger glasses are much more impressive-looking and steak houses are havens for client entertaining. However, if the same amount of wine is poured in a larger glass, it looks like less wine, so they pour more.

I'm not saying they are doing it on purpose to deceive you; quite the opposite. They do it because the larger glasses are more impressive and the restaurant feels they are providing more value to their customers. And perhaps they are. Just bear this in mind when going to restaurants where you see large glasses.

Also be cognizant of the type of wine that you are having. Five ounces is not a standard drink for all wines. The higher the alcohol in the wine, the less it will take to equal one standard drink. One glass of California Zinfandel at 14.8 percent alcohol would equal almost twice the number of standard drinks of a German Riesling at 8 percent alcohol. So be careful of that, too.

ARE YOU A SUPERTASTER?

Supertasters do exist. Although there are a small number of them, they do live among us.

Before you think these are people with superhuman abilities, though, all we mean by "supertasters" is that they have a heightened sense of taste because they have more taste buds. These are sometimes the very picky eaters that have to have everything "on the side" when you go out because they are so sensitive. They don't like spice, they don't like anything with a hint of bitterness. We really should call them by their actual name: hyper tasters.

People fall into three categories of tasters—the hyper tasters (or supertasters), the tasters, and the non-tasters—depending on the number of taste buds each has on their tongue. Hyper tasters have more taste buds on their tongue than the average person and non-tasters have fewer taste buds than average. Hyper tasters are much more sensitive to flavors and textures while non-tasters are not really sensitive at all. All the rest are known simply as tasters.

I once dated a guy who always had to have his food spicy when dining out, and not just spicy, we are talking nuclear! Knowing what I know now, he probably was a non-taster. He likely needed the intensity in order to perceive the taste.

WANT TO FIND OUT IF YOU ARE A SUPERTASTER?

Take blue food coloring, a piece of paper with a seven-millimeter-wide hole punched into it, and a magnifying glass.

Step 1: Dab a cotton swab with the blue food coloring on the tip of your tongue. The tongue will take up the dye, but the papillae (the tiny structures that house the taste buds) will stay pink.

Step 2: Put the piece of paper with the hole on the front part of your tongue.

Step 3: Count the number of pink dots inside the hole, using the magnifying glass.

» Under 15 papillae = non-taster

» Over 30 papillae = hyper taster

» Tasters are everything else in between.

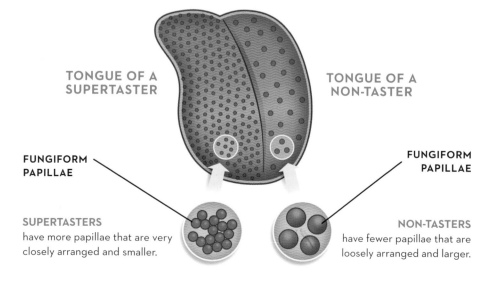

TONGUE OF A
SUPERTASTER

TONGUE OF A
NON-TASTER

FUNGIFORM
PAPILLAE

FUNGIFORM
PAPILLAE

SUPERTASTERS
have more papillae that are very
closely arranged and smaller.

NON-TASTERS
have fewer papillae that are
loosely arranged and larger.

TASTER POPULATION

NON-TASTERS
25 PERCENT

TASTERS
50 PERCENT

SUPERTASTERS
25 PERCENT

I have heard a wide range of figures on the number of hyper tasters and non-tasters, anywhere from 9 to 25 percent at both ends of the spectrum. What we do know is that the majority of people fall into the taster group and a small portion of the population are either hyper tasters or non-tasters. Having said that, women are more likely to be hyper tasters than men, and there are certain Asian and African ethnicities that have more hyper tasters as well.

THE FIVE S'S OF TASTING WINE

O YOU EVER PAY ATTENTION TO HOW YOU TASTE WINE? For most of us, especially when we're at a party or function where wine is served, there is only one step. Drink. We are at the bar, we order our glass, and we kick it back. Done.

Perhaps you have seen others getting into it a bit more than that. They tilt their glass to look at the color, swirl it around, smell inside the glass, take a small taste, and make slurping sounds.

To an outsider this may look incredibly snobby or pedantic or like showing off (and for some people, all those things might be true). However, the overall purpose behind these steps of tasting wine "properly" is to taste more flavors and get the most out of every sip.

In order to do this you will need to take a step back, take your time, and pay attention to what your senses are telling you. There are five steps to tasting wine, which I call the Five S's, and each of these steps has its own objective.

If you put all of these steps together, you get much more out of the experience than if you just kick it back.

The Five S's of tasting wine are:

1. See
2. Swirl
3. Sniff
4. Sip
5. Savor

HOW TO PROPERLY HOLD A GLASS

Before we get to the Five S's we need to discuss the way to hold a wineglass. It may sound silly, but there is a point and it is a pet peeve of mine, especially when I see people do it incorrectly in movies and TV shows. Many people hold their wineglass up toward the top with their fingers around the bulbous part of the glass. This may be how you hold a water glass, but it is *not* how you want to hold a wineglass. Why? Well, in addition to getting ugly fingerprints on your glass, your body temperature changes the wine.

Your body is much warmer than the wine (white or red) and your hand will heat the liquid in the glass much faster than if you hold it at the stem. Warm wine tastes less fruity and your palate then focuses more on the alcohol. Alcohol compounds are released at a faster rate at warmer temperatures, and the wine tastes more alcoholic and possibly more bitter to your palate.

This is why wineglasses have stems. Holding the wineglass by the stem allows the wine to stay at a more constant temperature so you can enjoy it longer.

Holding the glass by the stem can also prevent it from slipping out of your hand. I usually hold the wine stem toward the base with my pinky finger under the base. This helps me have a firmer grip on the glass, especially if I have to wade through a crowd at a party. I keep more wine in my glass than on my clothes. No joke; before I learned this principle, I went to one party where I spilled wine three times on myself and other guests (and this was before I'd had anything to drink).

THE FIRST S—"SEE"

Many of us are very dependent on what we see. We train our eyes probably better than any of our senses. But how can that help us with wine?

Seeing is an important part of the process of tasting wine because a wine's color can tell us a lot about how the wine will taste. The color can indicate the wine's richness, its condition, and the types of flavors we might get.

I've seen people hold their glass up to the light to look at the color. While it is good that they are taking note of the color, this is not the best way to do this. There are reflections and other light sources that interfere and influence the color of the wine when you hold it up to the light.

To best look at a wine's color, tilt the glass over a white surface. This could mean using the white tablecloth at a restaurant or a white napkin. By tilting the glass over a white surface, you get the true color of the wine.

Notice, too, the color in the center of the glass (what we call the meniscus) and the color where the wine hits the edge of the glass (which we call the rim). Some wines have a consistent color from meniscus to rim. Others are much paler at the rim.

Certain grape varieties, such as Cabernet Sauvignon, have thick skin. The thicker the skin of the grape, the deeper the color of the wine. This is because there is more pigmentation in the skin to color the wine. Grape varieties with a thin skin, such as Pinot Noir, are much paler in color. If you tilt the glass over the fingers of your other hand (the one not holding the glass), and you can't see your fingers through the wine at the meniscus or towards the rim, chances are that it's a dense and concentrated wine. That doesn't necessarily mean it's better quality, it just means it's more dense.

Generally speaking, grape varieties with thicker skins (and deeper color) also tend to have a higher level of tannin or bitterness. If you cannot handle a ton of bitterness, a deep color may indicate a wine that will be too tannic and bitter for your preference.

Wines that are youthful have a bright color. However, wines change color as they age. White wines get darker in color while red wines lose their color. As both white wines and red wines age, they go toward the more orange and brownish hues. If you like very fruity, youthful wines, a wine with a pale color with orange or brownish hues may indicate a mature wine whose flavors you may not like.

Color can also indicate faults in wines. Have you ever cut open a fresh apple and left it on the counter for a few minutes? It turns brown. That's the process of oxidation. Oxygen molecules come in, change some of the chemical compounds, and change the color, aromas, and flavors. In wine this will also indicate that the fruity aromas and flavors will be diminished and that there will be more nutty aromas (or, worse, sherry or vinegar-like aromas).

"GREAT LEGS!"

You may have seen people swirl their glass and say this, indicating great-quality wine. What they mean by "legs" are the small, teardrop-like streams that fall back toward the middle of the glass when you swirl the wine and then stop. It is a myth that legs have anything to do with quality. They actually have more to do with the level of alcohol. The higher the alcohol in the wine, the more viscous it is, which results in thicker "legs."

If you have a wine that is young, say under three years old, that is intended to be consumed for its youthful fruitiness, but it has a brownish hue, this could be a sign that the wine is oxidized. An unintentionally oxidized wine is a fault.

Identifying a fault like this can help save you from an embarrassing situation in front of clients or from a bad bottle at a restaurant. In chapter 11, we will talk about how to properly send a wine back. In this instance, it is the color that can tip you off that it might be a faulty wine.

The first S—See—is an important step. Make sure you take the time to use your eyes and make observations about what it is that you are looking at. It may help you understand what you taste and could help you save face and money.

THE SECOND S—"SWIRL"

Swirling is the next step in tasting wine appropriately. Swirling a glass may look cool to some people or like showing off to others, but it has a very important purpose. It's also important to do it well so you don't fling wine everywhere.

In the last chapter, we spoke about how the nose can perceive approximately two hundred compounds in wine. Some of these compounds are more volatile than others. When I say "volatile," I don't mean they are going to explode. Volatile compounds are those that are more unstable and therefore are released into the air more easily than others.

The less volatile compounds are stronger in their chemical bonds, or perhaps heavier, and are not released as easily, and are therefore less likely to be picked up by our receptors. Remember, in order for any aroma to be perceived, it needs to be released into the air and travel up our nasal cavity to where our aroma receptors are.

The simple act of swirling the wine around in the glass releases more of these compounds into the air. Therefore, more swirling = more perceived aromas.

You may be scared of spilling wine when swirling. If you are, do what I did (and still do sometimes) and follow these steps:

1. *Pour wine in your glass about a quarter to one-half way.* This
   leaves plenty of room in the glass to swirl and not spill. This is
   easy to do when you are home. However, this is not so easy at
   restaurants where they generally fill the wineglass to the top.
   You may luck out as many more restaurants are using five-
   to-six-ounce carafes to measure, serve, and pour wine. I like
   getting the most out of my wine-tasting experience, so when
   I see these small carafes coming to the table I generally ask to
   pour the wine myself. Yes, they look at me strangely, but this
   way I get to pour the amount of wine I want so that I can swirl
   with abandon.

2. *Keep the wineglass on the table and hold the glass near the bottom of the stem.* Again, you do not want to hold the glass by the top, bulbous part. Your hand will warm up the wine and that will change the way you perceive the wine (see page 34).

3. *With the glass still on the table, make circles using the base of the glass so that the wine inside the glass swirls around.* As time goes by you will feel comfortable enough that you will be able to swirl the wine in the glass while holding it in your hand and not on the table. I often still swirl on the table, though.

If you still have your doubts, try this test the next time you have a glass of wine.

Step 1: Immediately after a glass of wine has been poured, and with no swirling, pick it up and smell the wine.

Step 2: Swirl the glass and then smell the wine.

Notice a difference? You should get more aromas. That's why we do it!

Again, aromas are flavors. Therefore, the more aromas we perceive, the more flavors we perceive. The more flavors we perceive, the more enjoyable the experience (provided that you like those flavors).

THE THIRD S—"SNIFF"

We discussed the importance of smell and how we smell in the last chapter, and we just discussed how to get more aromas out of the wine by swirling it. Now it's time that we actually smell it.

Sniffing for me consists of three separate stages. I call it my Chest, Chin, Nose Test to see how aromatic the wine is and to identify different aromas at each stage. Is it absolutely necessary? Not at all. But I get more out of the experience when I do it this way.

CHEST

Hold the wine at your chest. Some very aromatic grape varieties (such as Muscat) can be smelled here. The aromatic compounds that reach your nose from here are the most volatile, so they will be different than the ones that you will be able to smell when the glass is at your chin or nose. I find the aromas that I can smell from my chest are the most fruity.

CHIN

Now hold the wineglass to your chin. Do you smell any more than you did at your chest? Do you smell different types of aromas? You smell much more intense fruit here, but you may be able to pick up other types of aromas—perhaps floral and herbal, or nutty.

NOSE

Finally, stick your nose in the glass. And I do mean this literally. Stick your nose right inside the glass and take a big sniff without snorting any wine (don't laugh, I did that once!). I sometimes find one nostril is more receptive than another. I will then tilt my glass toward the more receptive nostril so that I can smell more intricate aromas. It may work for you, too. It may also look more subtle if it bothers you to stick your nose all the way in the glass.

Additionally, try different ways to bring air in through your nose when you sniff. Some people find a large sniff that they can hear gets the most aromas. Others find a long, slow, and silent sniff works better. Try different techniques to see what works best for your nose. This is about you and getting the most out of your experience.

Some grape varieties are fairly neutral. You probably will not be able to smell anything until you stick your nose inside the glass. Chardonnay, for example, is a grape variety that is much more neutral in its characteristics than, say, Sauvignon Blanc or Riesling. This is especially true for Chardonnay that does not see any oak in the winemaking process (for example, many Bourgogne Blancs or Chablis). It's not very aromatic. This is why you often see Chardonnay fermented and aged in oak, which adds more vanilla and spice aromatic complexity to the wine.

The more layers of aromas you smell, the more complex the wine. You may have heard people say, "This is a very complex wine." What they mean is that they don't get just fruity aromas, but a wide spectrum of aromas with many layers of flavor (fruit, vanilla, toast, butter, minerals, etc.).

You may not smell many layers of aromas right away. In the beginning you may register just "wine." That's OK. But take the time to see what your nose is telling you. The more you pay attention, the more it will tell you and the more enjoyment you will get out of it.

THE FOURTH S—"SIP"

Ah, now comes most people's favorite part—sipping the wine.

In the last chapter we spoke of the different tastes your tongue can perceive: sweet, sour, salt, bitter, and umami. As you'll recall, wine really has only sweet, sour, and bitter, so at least that makes things easier.

Have you ever noticed that people take different-size sips? I have conducted tastings where people are amazingly timid about tasting wine. Some people take a sip that reminds me of a five-year-old taking a molecule-size taste of Brussels sprouts. Come on people, this is wine!

You need to make sure you have enough wine in your mouth for your taste buds to perceive all the flavors. Take about a tablespoonful in your mouth and roll it around your tongue. This way you are getting every taste bud to wake up and take notice of the wine.

Rolling the wine around your mouth also aerates the wine and warms it up, releasing more aromatic compounds that you perceive as flavors. If you just kick the wine back, you will not get anywhere near the experience. Again, try it for yourself. Take a sip of wine, kick it back, don't think about it. Wait a few minutes. Then take a sip, roll it around, hold it in your mouth for a few seconds before you swallow it. I bet you will notice a ton more flavor.

Also take note of the weight and texture of the wine in your mouth. If you don't think you can tell the difference, think about this. If I asked you if you could tell the difference in your mouth between skim milk, whole milk, and heavy cream, you most likely could. The same is true for wine. Some wines are light and delicate while others are quite heavy and dense.

You may not have noticed wine's weight or texture before. With every new wine you taste, take notice. You may realize that you like the flavor of a wine but are not fond of its weight. This will help you choose wines later on by pinpointing your preferences.

Want to get even more flavor? Try this:

» Take about a tablespoon in your mouth.
» While holding the wine in your mouth, purse your lips like you are going to kiss someone on the cheek and suck in air through your mouth (kind of like a reverse whistle).
» Make sure the air is circulating with the wine so that you are making a sound (this sound sort of reminds me of a bird chirping).
» Then roll it around your tongue again and then swallow.

Did you get more then? Of course! By doing this you are getting even more oxygen into the wine, breaking apart more aromatic compounds for you to perceive. It may look and sound silly to you, but this is how professional wine tasters do their job. It helps them get more aromas and flavors and it will help you, too.

THE FIFTH S—"SAVOR"

You might think that savoring a wine is part of sipping, but it's not. It's really its own separate stage, and a very important one. This is the time to really reflect on what you have just tasted. This is when you let your brain pick apart the wine in a split second and tell you whether you like it or not.

Understand, though, that there is a difference between saying "I like this wine" and "It's a quality wine." Sometimes they are the same, but sometimes not. Savoring is the step where both of these statements are deciphered.

Professional tasters use this time to analyze a wine's quality (hopefully putting aside personal preference). When I was taking the Master of Wine exam, I ran through twelve parameters in my head to determine each wine's quality level. Let me introduce you to three of them that will put you well on your way to teaching your palate to identify a quality wine.

BALANCE

In the last chapter we spoke about what the tongue can perceive. The tongue picks up the levels of acidity, alcohol, tannin, and weight, while the nose is able to detect the levels of fruitiness and flavor. Balance is achieved in a wine when all of these elements—fruit, acidity, alcohol, tannin, and weight—are fairly equal so that no one thing sticks out like a sore thumb.

Sometimes one of the elements does stand out quite heavily. For example, some wines from warm or hot climates have very high levels of alcohol. Having high alcohol by itself is not necessarily a bad thing if the other elements match up to it. However, when the alcohol overpowers everything else and you taste predominantly heat and bitterness in the aftertaste, then it is said to be "unbalanced" or "hot" (as alcohol can register as heat on your palate—see page 28).

Imagine listening to a large symphony orchestra playing a piece of classical music. If the horns overpower the delicate violins, or if the percussion is way too loud, it sounds disconnected. However, when they are all in balance, no instrument stands out. The orchestra becomes one harmonious unit. The same is true for a wine.

LENGTH

When you savor a wine after you have taken a sip, how long does the flavor last? Ten seconds? Thirty seconds? One minute? Five minutes? The time span the flavor lasts in your mouth is called a wine's "length." The amount of time varies from person to person. If it lasts a long time (relative to other wines), then we say it has "long length." If the flavor is quite brief, we say the length is "short." A longer length indicates a higher-quality wine. However, I should add a caveat to that: the flavor should be pleasant, not flawed.

Given that our palates are quite different, start to take note of how long flavors last on your palate. You will begin to see the difference among wines. This can help you spot better value wines, especially in the same price range.

COMPLEXITY

Complexity in wine is like complexity in an ice cream sundae. You may like plain vanilla ice cream, but imagine it now with hot fudge. Do you like it more? Then you layer it with toasted nuts, then chocolate chips and peanut butter chips. How about now? Then you put whipped cream and a cherry on top. When you build an ice cream sundae you are layering flavors for a bigger impact.

The same is true for wine. When a wine has many layers of flavors we say the wine is "complex." When all we taste is just the plain vanilla (meaning all we get is one flavor, such as fruit), then we say it is "simple" or "one-dimensional." More layers (complexity) indicates a higher-quality wine. Having said that, the flavors should complement one another. After all, you wouldn't want tomato sauce on your ice cream sundae, would you?

Wineries create complexity in their wines in many ways. They can pick different types of grape varieties or grapes from varied locations, each with its own unique characteristics, and blend them together. They can ferment and/or age their wines in different types of oak with different toast levels for varied lengths of time. Oak can add flavors of spice, nut, caramel, butterscotch and wood. Oak is therefore used as a "complexing" agent.

Oak aromas and flavors include:

» Flavors from aging in French oak: vanilla, nutmeg, cinnamon;
» Flavors from aging in American oak: coconut, vanilla, tobacco;
» Flavors can also vary depending on how the barrel was toasted on the inside while it was being made. The higher the toast, the more intense the flavor, and some taste like smoke (similar to the smokiness you can taste on bacon).

Balance, length, and complexity are quality parameters, each with its own purpose. These parameters are also somewhat more objective than personal preferences as they can, to a degree, be measured. How long do the flavors last? Does the level of alcohol overpower the level of fruit? And which aromas or flavors are detected?

It can be quite difficult, however, to separate your personal preferences from your quality assessment of a wine.

For example, let's say you do not like oaked Chardonnay (meaning a Chardonnay that was fermented and/or aged in oak barrels). However, you notice that the flavor lasts a long time on your palate, the wine is in balance, and it has many aromas (fruit, vanilla, spice, cream, minerals, etc.). If you look at the whole picture of the wine, including these more objective parameters, you may see that it is a high-quality wine. You may just not like the style or flavors of the wine.

I've heard people say, "You can get a $5 wine that's just as good as a $100 one." While I understand the logic of "I can buy twenty of the $5 bottles for just one bottle of the $100," saying it is better quality is just silly. While you may prefer the $5 bottle for its flavors and drinkability (and wallet-friendly appeal), understand that a $100 wine is a $100 wine for a reason and should taste as such.

There are more parameters of quality, but these three—balance, length, and complexity—are the ones used most by wine professionals and critics. So they will do you just fine. They will help you detect and taste better-quality wines. Learning quality parameters will help you find wine whose flavors you like, and *that* represents good value for the money.

A SECRET SIXTH S—"SPITTING"

For those of you who are interested in professional tasting, spitting is another important S. You might be thinking "Spitting? Ew! That's disgusting!" or "What a waste of good wine!" Spitting, however, has an important purpose for the professional taster.

Professional tasters spit to not get drunk, especially when they have a large number of wines to taste in one sitting. I go to tastings all the time with hundreds of wines. When judging at wine competitions, it is not unusual for me to taste more than a hundred wines in a few hours. I was in Germany at a trade tasting a few years back and there were over three hundred wines available to taste in one day. If I did not spit, they would have had to carry me out after my sixth wine (the pours are small).

Having said that, a little alcohol still gets into your bloodstream through the walls of your mouth even when you spit the wine out. Additionally, you always manage to swallow some residual wine. So even when you spit you have to be careful.

If you sign up for a wine class, or have your own wine-tasting party, I would recommend learning how to spit. Don't be surprised, though, if it takes some practice. When I went to my first wine-tasting class I ended up spitting wine on my lap and getting some on the person sitting next to me in the process.

Wine tasting classes have spittoons and generally they will provide a small plastic cup to spit in as well. Spit in the small cup and then dump the spit cup into the larger spittoon. This will prevent any mishaps like I had.

THE ONE MINUTE WINE MASTER QUIZ

THIS CHAPTER WILL TAKE YOU THROUGH THE KEYS to finding your wine preferences. It will help you to identify wines that you will like time after time. It can also help you find wines for your friends, sweetheart, colleagues, and many others.

You will see three things that will help you here:

1. *The One Minute Wine Master* Quiz
2. *The One Minute Wine Master* Answer Wheel
3. *The One Minute Wine Master* Cheat Sheet

HOW DOES IT WORK?

This quiz works like any other multiple-choice quiz except that each answer has a number of points associated with it. You will need to tally your number of points as you go along. If you have ever taken a *Cosmopolitan* magazine quiz, you will know how to do this.

At the end of the quiz, add up your total score. Then look to the key to find your wine-preference category. Your total score will place you in one of four categories: Spring, Summer, Fall, or Winter. Each season has its own set of characteristics, just as zodiac signs have their own traits. Once you have your season, go to *The One Minute Wine Master* Answer Wheel to see what wines fit your new profile. It's that easy!

WILL IT REALLY TAKE ONLY ONE MINUTE?

There are eleven questions in *The One Minute Wine Master* Quiz and, as the name suggests, it should take you under a minute to complete. Unless, of course, you are one of those people who agonize over answering questions. But even then it probably won't take you more than two minutes.

Don't think too much! It's actually better if you choose quickly; do not think too much about each question, and let your subconscious choose. This is designed to get your first impressions. Thinking too much defeats the purpose. I want you to enjoy more and think less.

This is the chapter for those people who want to cut to the chase, get their information and go. That's great! Just take *The One Minute Wine Master* Quiz, look at *The One Minute Wine Master* Answer Wheel with your category's wines, and that's it! No memorizing anything, no explanations. You are off to the store with a list of wines that will very likely suit your personal palate!

I have found, though, that the more people find out about wine and their individual style preferences, the more they want to know. When we know more, we understand more, we appreciate more, and we can share with friends and family more. That's why I encourage you to read the chapters that explain why *The One Minute Wine Master* works, and the summary on each seasonal category, and the descriptions of the types of wines that fit those categories.

There are also helpful hints for people who may find that their results are not aligned with their personal preferences. To take full advantage of *The One Minute Wine Master*, you will find it helpful to read the other chapters. However, it's totally up to you.

WHAT IF I WANT TO DO THE QUIZ MORE THAN ONCE OR FOR OTHER PEOPLE?

You're in luck! In the back of the book there are three additional quizzes for you or your friends to do. After that, you will have to do what most people do with *Cosmo* quizzes—write your answers on a separate paper, add them up, and see what your score is. Or you can go to www.everydaywineguide.com and do this online.

THE ONE MINUTE WINE MASTER QUIZ

QUESTION	3 POINTS
1. How do you take your coffee or tea?	Black/nothing added
2. How much sugar do you add to your coffee or tea?	None
3. What type of chocolate do you prefer?	Dark, bitter chocolate
4. How often do you put lemon on your fish?	Never
5. What is your favorite juice?	Apple
6. How spicy do you like your food?	Extremely hot
7. If you compare the body of a white wine to the body of heavy cream, whole milk, or skim milk, which would you prefer?	Heavy cream
8. If you compare the body of a red wine to the body of heavy cream, whole milk, or skim milk, which would you prefer?	Heavy cream
9. What type of perfume or cologne do you like?	Spicy/intense
10. What type of gum do you prefer?	Spicy (cinnamon)
11. What is your favorite snack?	Something rich like chocolate or a candy bar

KEY

SPRING: 1–13 POINTS
SUMMER: 14–19 POINTS
FALL: 20–25 POINTS
WINTER: 26–33 POINTS

2 POINTS	1 POINT	0 POINTS	TALLY POINTS
A little milk or cream	A lot of milk or cream	I don't drink coffee or tea	
A teaspoon	Two or more teaspoons	I don't drink coffee or tea	
Milk chocolate	White Chocolate	I don't eat or like chocolate	
Sometimes	Always	I don't eat fish	
Orange	Lemonade	I don't drink juice	
Medium	Mild	None	
Whole milk	Skim milk		
Whole milk	Skim milk		
Sweet/candied	Floral/fresh	I don't like perfume or cologne	
Bubble gum or fruity gum	Fresh (mint, violet, etc.)	I don't chew gum	
Something savory like chips or crackers	Something light like a piece of fruit or carrot sticks	None of these	

TOTAL POINTS

THE ONE MINUTE WINE MASTER
ANSWER WHEEL

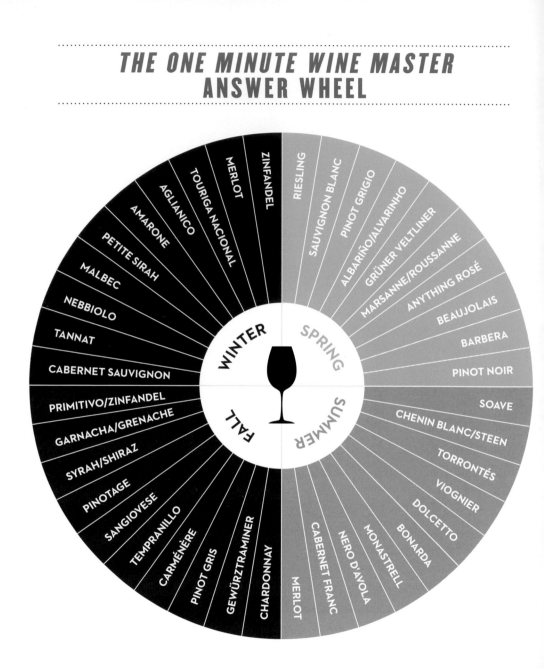

THE ONE MINUTE WINE MASTER
CHEAT SHEET

SPRING

Those in the Spring category prefer wines that are delicate, pure, and crisp, with floral, herbal, or lightly fruity aromas and flavors. To a Spring, wines in the other categories are just a bit too much. Springs like their wines refreshing. Springs' preferences:

- » Concentration: light
- » Tannin (bitterness and structure): none to low
- » Alcohol tolerance: light
- » Acidity preference: high
- » Sweetness preference: varies

SUMMER

Summers love obvious fruit in their wines, but don't like the spiciness, bitterness, weight, or heavier texture that Falls and, especially, Winters prefer. Summers are attracted to softer textures, but find some of the delicate, fresh wines that Springs enjoy to be too dilute or sour or sweet. Summers' preferences:

- » Concentration: medium
- » Tannin (bitterness and structure): low to medium
- » Alcohol tolerance: varies
- » Acidity preference: medium
- » Sweetness preference: dry—no sweetness

FALL

Falls aren't attracted to the intensity of weight, bitterness, or alcohol that Winters enjoy. However, they want a little more concentration and density than Summers. Additionally, those in the Fall category enjoy spice whereas Springs and Summers generally like it less. Falls' preferences:

» Concentration: medium to medium high
» Tannin (bitterness and structure): medium to medium high
» Alcohol tolerance: medium to medium high
» Acidity preference: varies
» Sweetness preference: dry—no sweetness

WINTER

Winters tend toward big, rich, full-bodied and powerful, high-octane wines. The wines they enjoy are characterized by intensity, strength, high levels of alcohol and tannin (bitterness), and full body. Winters' preferences:

» Concentration: high
» Tannin (bitterness and structure): high
» Alcohol tolerance: high
» Acidity preference: varies
» Sweetness preference: dry—no sweetness

WHY THE ONE MINUTE WINE MASTER *WORKS*

THE QUESTIONS IN *THE ONE MINUTE WINE MASTER* QUIZ are seemingly unrelated to wine. However, each question relates to something specific in wine and to your palate's reaction to those elements. Combining all of these reactions helps create a picture of your wine style.

Let's take a closer look at each question to see what your answers suggest about your preferences in wine.

1. HOW DO YOU TAKE YOUR COFFEE OR TEA?

This question addresses your tolerance for bitterness.

Have you ever tasted coffee or black tea without any milk? Both coffee and tea have a chemical in them that can make them taste bitter. This chemical

> ❝ *Springs are the least tolerant of bitterness.*

is called tannin and it creates a drying, bitter, and sometimes astringent sensation in your mouth. Tannin is also found in some wines, especially red wines.

People vary in their tannin tolerance. To some, black coffee can taste slightly bitter. To others, the bitterness is overwhelming and tastes very drying and astringent.

When milk is added to black tea or coffee, a chemical reaction takes place between the protein in the milk and the tannin, which makes the coffee or tea softer on your palate and less bitter. Offsetting bitterness is one of the main reasons milk is added to these beverages in the first place.

Out of all *The One Minute Wine Master* categories, Springs are the least tolerant of bitterness. They will put the most milk or cream in their coffee or tea to reduce its bitterness.

Winters, on the opposite end of the spectrum, generally take their coffee or tea with no milk or cream. Winters have the highest tolerance for tannin, bitterness, or astringency. Not much tastes too bitter for them.

Summers and Falls fall between these two extremes. Summers are closer to Springs than Fall, so they are more tolerant to liking tannin than Springs, but less so than Falls. Falls can handle more tannins in their wines than Springs or Summers, though not as much as Winters.

2. HOW MUCH SUGAR DO YOU ADD TO YOUR COFFEE OR TEA?

This question addresses your tolerance for bitterness and sweetness.

Sugar does not react chemically with bitterness the way milk does in coffee or tea. Although it doesn't take tannin away, sugar masks bitterness so the beverage may seem less bitter to you. It distracts your palate from the tannin by giving it something sweet to focus on.

These first two questions tell me quite a bit about the types of wines you are likely to prefer. However, some people have a cup of joe because they use it to get up in the morning. It's all about the caffeine boost. They don't really enjoy it or taste it. If that is you, consider your tolerance for bitterness and sweetness in other things that you eat or drink to answer these questions.

This question may also confuse people who take a ton of cream and sugar in their coffee because their office coffee is awful. I have tasted some office coffees that were so bad that I needed maximum sugar and milk to make it drinkable. Others have just gotten used to having their coffee that way, not realizing that their palates have changed.

These questions were designed to identify your tolerance for sweetness and bitterness, so it's important to understand your preferences. Think about your tolerance and answer the questions appropriately for the most accurate results.

People also vary in their tolerance for sweetness even in the complete absence of bitterness. Springs tend to have a higher tolerance for sweeter wines. If you need two or more teaspoons of sugar in your tea or coffee, chances are you have a higher tolerance for sweetness and a lower tolerance for bitterness.

This is not to imply that all Springs prefer sweet wines. You may prefer dry wines that also have crisp acidity and a refreshing palate. However, Springs' taste buds have a higher tolerance for sugar than the other season's do.

If you take your coffee or tea with no sugar, you may have a low preference for sugar in your beverages. This could also mean you can take bitterness. Winters have the highest tolerance for bitterness of any season. Again, Summers and Falls are somewhere in the middle, with Falls leaning toward Winters and Summers leaning toward Springs.

3. WHAT TYPE OF CHOCOLATE DO YOU PREFER?

Most people love the flavor of chocolate, but as we discussed in previous chapters, flavor has more to do with your nose than your tongue. The level of cocoa in chocolate, however, is what can make it bitter. Taste baking chocolate alongside a milk chocolate bar and you will see what I mean.

Dark chocolate, like cooking chocolate, has more cocoa in it and therefore more bitterness and less sweetness. If you prefer dark chocolate, your tolerance for bitterness is probably quite high, which would lean you more toward Fall and Winter. Springs do not prefer dark chocolate or even semisweet chocolate because they find them too bitter. Their bitterness receptors are much more active than, say, Winters'. Winters have a high level of tolerance for bitterness and neither black coffee nor dark bitter chocolate are unpleasant to their palates.

So does that mean if you like milk chocolate you are middle-of-the-road? I'm afraid it's not that simple. Milk chocolate has less cocoa powder and lots of sugar to mask the bitterness. Springs may like milk chocolate, but it may have more to do with the sweetness of the chocolate and flavor rather than the percentage of cocoa.

Sweet milk chocolate and white chocolate are the preferred chocolates of Springs. White chocolate is actually not chocolate at all because it has no cocoa in it. It's just cocoa butter, all creamy sweetness and no bitterness. Springs do not like dark, bitter chocolate. There are some dark chocolates with a ton of sweetness to compensate for the bitterness, but I'm talking about really dark chocolate here. Perhaps it's time for a taste test!

You may never have analyzed why you like chocolate before, so you may not know. For now, just know that if you are a dark chocolate person you can take bitterness. And white chocolate? Not so much.

4. HOW OFTEN DO YOU PUT LEMON ON YOUR FISH?

I'm sure many of you might say "sometimes" to this question because it depends on the fish. For example, you may always add lemon to fried shrimp but not shrimp cocktail or salmon. That's OK. If sometimes is your answer, then that's your answer.

Can you guess what this question is asking? Lemon is tart. Adding it to anything adds acidity. Some people have a high tolerance for acidity (which means they would generally always put lemon on their fish) while others find it unpleasant. This question is not the only acid indicator, which is why there are other questions below that address acidity tolerance.

Wine definitely has acidity. Some wines have very high acidity and others do not. So knowing your tolerance for acidity helps us figure out the kinds of wine you're likely to enjoy.

5. WHAT IS YOUR FAVORITE JUICE?

This is another acidity question. Citrus fruits generally have the highest acidity of the most common juices we grab in the supermarket, which is why lemonade is at the tartest end of the scale. We perceive apple juice as softer. This is why apple juice is at the other end of the spectrum. Orange juice seems like it's somewhere in the middle.

Those who prefer lemonade have a higher tolerance for tartness and acidity than those who prefer apple juice. Therefore, Springs would lean toward lemon juice while Falls and Winters would lean more toward apple juice.

6. HOW SPICY DO YOU LIKE YOUR FOOD?

There are no spices added to wine (except around the holidays in recipes for mulled wine). When you hear wines described as having aromas of spices such as black pepper, cinnamon, or nutmeg, it doesn't mean the winemaker added them in the winemaking process. Those aromas are reminiscent of these spices and come from chemicals found in the grape or from the barrels the wine was fermented and/or matured in.

However, this question is getting at your tolerance for alcohol more than at your enjoyment of spice (though it does that, too). High alcohol creates a thermal reaction in your mouth, which makes it taste "hot." In chapter 3, I mention the story of my first taste of whiskey and how it felt like a fire in my mouth. The same reaction happens with spice. If you have ever had super-nuclear-hot buffalo wings, you know what I mean. Your mouth is on fire, you feel the heat, and you start to sweat, maybe even tear up. Wine never gets *that* hot, but high alcohol in a wine does register as heat.

Some quiz takers have said "Well, I can handle hot foods; does that mean I should put down medium to extremely hot?" Not necessarily. You should answer this question based on how you prefer your food in general. If you need your food to be extremely hot in order to enjoy it then, yes, put down extremely hot as your answer. But, if you only order the extremely hot wings in front of your friends because you think it shows you can "take it," then I would consider revising your answer.

Those who do not tolerate spice well also generally do not prefer high-alcohol wines. It registers on their palates as too much heat, which makes it impossible for them to enjoy the wine. Those on the other end of the spectrum, who like it "the hotter the better," enjoy the heat of high-alcohol wines and don't think twice.

7 AND 8. IF YOU COMPARE THE BODY OF A WHITE WINE (RED WINE) TO THE BODY OF HEAVY CREAM, WHOLE MILK, OR SKIM MILK, WHICH WOULD YOU PREFER?

Pretty much everyone can tell the difference between skim milk, whole milk, and heavy cream, right? In the same way, one can perceive the body, weight, and texture differences between light-bodied, medium-bodied, and full-bodied wines. Similar concept.

Different grape varieties have different bodies and textures. For example, in general, Riesling is a light-bodied white wine, while Cabernet Sauvignon is a full-bodied red wine. Winemaking styles as well as climate can also have an impact on a wine's weight. This question helps narrow the field of grape varieties, styles, and winemaking regions.

9. WHAT TYPE OF PERFUME OR COLOGNE DO YOU LIKE?

This may seem like another odd question since you don't drink perfume. The purpose of this question is to identify the types of aromas you are attracted to.

Perfumes and colognes are combinations of aromas from many things. Most are a combination of different categories of scents—floral, sweet, candied, fruity, spicy, or woodsy.

However, there are many perfumes and colognes that are heavier in one category than another. For example, Estée Lauder Pleasures is made up of many floral scents. Included in this perfume are lilies, peonies, jasmine, and Baie rose. I would qualify this as a floral scent.

On the other end of the spectrum, Opium, by Yves Saint Laurent, does have some floral scents, but exotic spices are more prominent. Among other things, it has cloves, coriander, myrrh, cedar, and sandalwood blended in. I would consider this a heavier, more intense, spicy perfume.

Men's colognes are generally more intense and spicy in their scents, with cedar, bergamot, cardamom, and musk scents predominating. However, there are some that smell more aquatic and fresh (such as Davidoff Cool Water) or sweet (Ralph Lauren Polo Black, which has iced-mango notes) or spicy (such as Calvin Klein Obsession).

Sweet and candied scents smell just that way—like candy. Jessica Simpson came out with a brand of fragrance not too long ago, called Dessert, that had very candied aromas. One I remembered smelled like pure butter-cream icing. The Body Shop has a vanilla-scented body spray scent that smells very sweet. Some people love sweet fragrances while others may find them repulsive.

You may not know whether your favorite perfumes/colognes smell floral or sweet or spicy. If that's too hard, think of your favorite scents in general and answer the question based on those preferences.

Your answer to this question helps narrow the field again to identify wines that will be perfect for you. Some grape varieties are extremely aromatic and others are neutral in their aromas. Some grape varieties are extremely floral (such as Sauvignon Blanc) and others are more spicy (such as Syrah).

For some there may be a disconnect between the scents you like and what you will drink. Again, you don't drink perfumes or colognes. You may like spicy perfumes, but you don't necessarily like spicy foods or your wines with spicy flavors. That's OK. It's just to get you thinking. Knowing this may help you steer your answer toward wines that you will like.

10. WHAT TYPE OF GUM DO YOU PREFER?

This is similar to the previous question, except that you do put gum in your mouth.

If you prefer spicy gums, such as Wrigley's Big Red, that suggests you have a higher tolerance for spice, which could lean you toward Fall or Winter. Those who prefer bubble gum or fruit-flavored gums like grape, sour apple, cherry, etc., clearly like fruity flavors.

If you chose fresh, just keep in mind that I'm not asking you what gum you would use to freshen your breath after eating garlic. To get the most accurate response for your palate, you need to answer this question in terms of the types of gum you enjoy on a regular basis. If you always prefer minty-fresh gums (spearmint, peppermint, wintergreen) or even the floral/herbal kind (violet) over the others, that tells me you like tastes that are refreshing and delicate.

11. WHAT IS YOUR FAVORITE SNACK?

I find that people really fall into one of three snack camps—savory, fresh, or chocolate. Personally, I go for the savory: chips of any flavor, crackers, popcorn, nuts, or anything with salt and/or cheese. However, I know many chocoholics who crave only chocolate. Given a choice, what do you grab for at snack time?

This question helps define certain wine styles. For example, in some wines I find an herbal, savory quality that brings to mind a plate of pasta covered in a meaty tomato sauce.

Other wines have aromas and flavors of chocolate, vanilla, mocha, caramel—things you can find in a candy bar. And while I have yet to find a wine that smells of carrots or celery, there are many wines that are refreshing and almost feel healthy.

IS *THE ONE MINUTE WINE MASTER* FOOLPROOF?

The book that inspired me to write *The One Minute Wine Master* came out in the 1980s. It wasn't about wine; it was a book for women to simplify choosing cosmetics. *Color Me Beautiful* helped many to explore colors they might never have tried otherwise. Before I got this book I was fairly clueless about makeup and was doing the aqua blue eye shadow and fire engine red lipstick. Then again, I was only a teenager.

According to the book, I'm a Fall because I have brown hair and hazel eyes, which means fall colors and earth tones (brown, orange, etc.) should look good on me. And, forgive me for sounding a bit vain here, it does work—I think I do look great in those autumn earth tones.

However, does it work all the time and should I regard it as doctrine? Well, at the risk of seeming conceited, I think I really look good in rich purple, too. Purple was not one of my designated Fall colors. It's a Winter color, so does that mean the whole *Color Me Beautiful* system doesn't work? No. It gave me a starting point to feel comfortable and explore more. That is exactly what this book is designed to do. It's designed to give you a starting point to explore the incredibly complex world of wine and your own taste buds.

This quiz depends on a mathematical equation. So that means if you like the big, bold, tannic red wines of Winter yet you also like the delicate, crisp, sweet wines of Spring, the numbers may put you in the middle and characterize you as a Summer or a Fall.

How can you tell if this is the case? Take a look at your answers. For the question about the skim milk, whole milk, and heavy cream, did you say the same thing for both white and red? If not, that could be a clue that you may fit into different seasons for white and red. You may find that you're a Winter red, but a Spring white. That's OK, too.

Even if the quiz didn't work perfectly for you, *The One Minute Wine Master* Answer Wheel categories still might. Again, the quiz and wheel are designed to give you a starting point to say "Hey, I like these types of wines and I may be interested in trying these others that are in the same category."

CAN MY SEASONAL CATEGORY CHANGE?

Absolutely, as your tastes can change. My mom took cooking classes when I was six years old and for years after that she made quiche a lot. I hated quiche back then. Now, I love quiche! Our tastes change as we get older and are introduced to new flavors, new textures and tastes.

Your category can also change during the year. When the weather gets a little cooler, we gravitate to richer foods and we do the same with wine. During the summer months, we make lots of salads and lighter dishes (grilled chicken, fish, etc.) and we wait until the fall or winter for the heavier sauces and richer stews. It's the same thing with wine. You may find you enjoy Spring's white wines during May through August and a Fall's white wines from October through February (in the Northern Hemisphere, anyway).

You can feel free to jump into all the categories throughout the year. The quiz and wheel are guidelines. So have fun with it!

DOES WHERE I LIVE IMPACT MY PREFERENCES?

Possibly. Where you live can have an effect on the type of wine you prefer. I live in New York City. We have four distinct seasons. However, you may live in a warm climate where there is very little variation (e.g., southern Florida) or it's fairly cool (e.g., Maine). This is going to impact your preferences for sure. You may love spicy, rich wines in the Fall category, but when it's 100°F in the shade in Arizona, you probably want something light, crisp, and refreshing. If you live in northern Alaska, you may never want anything more delicate than red Zinfandel.

WHAT IF I LIKE IT ALL?

You may be the type of wine consumer who loves all wines and really doesn't have a strong preference. In this case, the quiz and the wheel may not help you identify a single category for you. However, the wheel will help you choose wines that you are in the mood for at a specific time or occasion.

Note: I have given this quiz to many people, and once I explain the reasoning behind the questions, some say "I want to change my answers." If this is you, feel free to go back, change your answers, and come up with a new score. Now that you know what each question is getting at, you can gear the answers more toward your specific palate for a more accurate result.

LEMON

GRAPEFRUIT

GREEN APPLE

FRESH-CUT GRASS

FLORAL

PALE HONEYCOMB

LILY

CANDY

LIME

SPRING

Spring is the season that reminds us of all things clean, fresh, crisp, floral, and bright. It's a season of delicate morning dew, flowers, and new tree blossoms. Those in the Spring category prefer wines that are fresh, bright, crisp, and delicate.

Your responses to the quiz suggest that you fall into the Spring category, which indicates that you may prefer wines at this soft, subtle, and gentle end of the spectrum.

Statements made by Springs that may correspond to your quiz answers:

» I don't drink coffee or black tea (it's too bitter) or I take coffee, but I generally like it light and sweet

» I don't like bitter chocolate

» I always have lemon on my fish, and I prefer lemonade to apple juice

» I generally don't like my food spicy (mildly spicy, if at all)

» I prefer lighter-bodied wines (generally whites more than reds)

» I prefer fresh, floral scents

» My favorite gums are minty or fresh

» I prefer fresh snacks such as fruit or carrots or celery sticks

Springs are at one end of *The One Minute Wine Master* spectrum—light, delicate, crisp, and floral. They are the opposite of Winters, who like full-bodied, robust, tannic, powerful wines. To Springs, Winters' wines are too high octane—too intense, too bitter, and/or too alcoholic. If you are a Spring, you generally prefer lightly fruity, crisp wines that are refreshing (and perhaps have a touch of sweetness).

Springs do not generally like a lot of spice in their food, if any at all. Their palates are too sensitive to it. For example, my mother is a Spring. I've always suspected even before she took the quiz. How? Every time we went out as a family for Mexican food, she would complain that the food was too spicy. Even mild guacamole seemed way too spicy to her and burned her tongue. She has a very low tolerance for spice. Even the slightest spice makes her feel like her mouth is on fire.

WINES SPRING MAY ENJOY

RIESLING (REE-sling)

Riesling is a delicate flower of a grape in a way. It is light in body and has high, crisp acidity—perfect for Springs. It is also highly perfumed, meaning it is very aromatic and often has floral aromas. It can have citrus flavors (lemon and lime) as well as stone fruit (such as peach, nectarine, apricot, etc.).

However, most people know Riesling as a sweet white wine. Sometimes it is. For example, Germany is famous for its delicious sweet Rieslings and they are available at practically every price point. Some of the regions in Germany famous for their Rieslings are Mosel, Rheingau, Pfalz, and Rheinhessen.

German Rieslings are also low in alcohol. To give you some perspective on what low means, for many wines 12 percent alcohol by volume is considered moderate. However, in Germany Rieslings made in a sweet style can be anywhere from 7 to 11 percent. This makes the wine seem even softer and gentler on your palate, which Springs can really appreciate.

Other regions have adopted this style. For example, some Rieslings from New Zealand share the German style—a little sweetness and modest alcohol.

Though there are some great inexpensive sweet Rieslings, you should not equate Riesling with "cheap" and "sweet." Alongside Cabernet Sauvignon, Pinot Noir, and Chardonnay, Riesling is considered a "noble" grape variety. It makes some of the longest-lived and most expensive wines in the world. It also demonstrates a sense of place quite well (see sidebar).

German wine labels can be very confusing. However, there is information on the label that can tell you how sweet it is.

SENSE OF PLACE

When we say a wine has a "sense of place" we mean that where it comes from is very evident in the taste and the style of the wine. The French term "terroir" refers to those climatic, topographical, and physical elements in the vineyard that create that wine's specific taste and sense of place.

Imagine for a moment that you could clone yourself (I have an identical twin, so I can imagine this very easily). Imagine that at birth one of you was sent to live in Brooklyn, one to the United Kingdom, one to Brazil, and one to Texas, and that you all meet up decades later for a reunion. All of you would have adapted to your environment. And, assuming you all spoke English, you likely picked up an accent, despite the fact that you are all genetically identical. Your genes haven't changed, just your accents. It's obvious where each of you lived. The accent you picked up is analogous to a wine's "sense of place."

Just like people, some grape varieties pick up these "accents" much more quickly and to a greater degree. Riesling is one of those grapes that shows more of a sense of place than others.

The following words on the label correspond to varying levels of sweetness:

NAME ON LABEL	PRONUNCIATION	SWEETNESS LEVEL
TROCKEN	TROCK-en	Dry (no sweetness at all)
QBA		Off-dry (slightly sweet)
KABINETT	cab-IH-net	Off-dry (slightly sweet) but higher quality than QbA
SPÄTLESE (means "late harvest")	SH-bate-LAY-zah	Sweeter than off-dry but not as sweet as auslese
AUSLESE (means "selected harvest")	OWSH-LAY-zah	Sweet

Riesling is the little darling of many sommeliers and my wine geek friends, in part because it pairs with more types of food than any other wine variety, from delicate seafood to spicy kung pao chicken.

On the opposite end of the style spectrum of German Riesling is the dry style made in Austria and Australia (particularly the Clare Valley and Eden Valley in South Australia). These wines are also light-bodied, but they are completely bone dry, so the acidity stands out a bit more and the alcohol is in the 12 to 14 percent range, depending on where the wine is grown.

Australian Rieslings are dry, though very fruity in aromas and on the palate, with strong lime fruit character. On the other hand, Old World Rieslings tend to have a

Note on aging Riesling: As Riesling ages, especially German Rieslings, it can take on a diesel aroma. Yes, you read correctly, diesel, as in kerosene. This is not necessarily a bad thing! In the wine industry, we often look for that aroma in older Riesling. It makes the wine unique. However, when you age white wines they gain color and spice and richness. In other words, they turn into wines that the Fall category may prefer.

mineral aroma (some people say this aroma smells like wet limestone, or the pavement after a spring rain). This Old World minerality tends to make the wine taste quite fresh and clean even though it is not as obviously fruity as wines from the New World (anyplace outside Europe).

DR. THANISCH RIESLING, KABINETT, BERNKASTELER BADSTUBE, MOSEL, GERMANY
Pale straw color with intense aromas of citrus, peaches, and steely minerality. On the palate it is slightly sweet with low alcohol and fresh crisp acidity. Well balanced.

PENFOLDS DRY RIESLING, EDEN VALLEY, SOUTH AUSTRALIA, AUSTRALIA
Pale straw yellow color with intense aromas of citrus fruits and especially ripe limes, floral notes of acacia, and a hint of honey. On the palate it is dry with racy (very crisp) acidity and a refreshingly clean, fruity finish.

SAUVIGNON BLANC (SAW-veen-yon BLONK)

Like Riesling, Sauvignon Blanc is an incredibly aromatic white grape variety. It also has refreshingly crisp acidity, giving it some "zing." However, you generally don't see wines made from 100 percent Sauvignon Blanc made in a sweet style, and the aromas are very different from Riesling. Springs will like Sauvignon Blanc because it is generally light-bodied, crisp, aromatic, and floral.

Sauvignon Blanc can have fruit aromas from citrus (lemon and grapefruit) to richer, more tropical aromas like passion fruit, kiwi, banana, pineapple, and fresh figs. The variation depends on where the grape is grown.

Sauvignon Blanc can smell quite floral, but it also has aromas that can be green. What do I mean by green? When you put your nose in a glass of

Sauvignon Blanc you will notice aromas that remind you of something "green" that can range from herbs to fresh-cut grass or to something more like asparagus.

Sauvignon Blanc originally comes from the Loire Valley, in France, and Sancerre and Pouilly-Fumé are the most famous places in the Loire for this grape. Sauvignon Blanc made there is quite citrusy and has a strong minerality. "Fumé" means "smoked" in French, and the mineral aromas in Pouilly-Fumé are often characterized as "gunflint." The same variety grown elsewhere doesn't have that gunflint aroma, though. Sauvignon Blanc also shows a strong "sense of place" (see the Sense of Place sidebar on page 71).

You can't talk about Sauvignon Blanc without mentioning its most infamous benchmark aroma: cat pee. Yes, you read correctly, cat pee, as in cat urine. The old British descriptor for great Loire Sauvignon Blanc was "cat's pee on a gooseberry bush." Not sure how anyone correctly identified that smell! Today, however, I don't see too many people describing Sauvignon Blanc with cat pee metaphors. Sauvignon Blancs can be quite pungent, but I can't say I've noticed many that reminded me of cat pee. Then again, I don't have a cat and am not particularly attuned to their bodily fluids.

Loire Valley Sauvignon Blancs are often aromatic, but New Zealand and South African Sauvignon Blancs are positively pungent. They are much more tropical in their aromas (more like passion fruit than citrus).

The style of Sauvignon Blancs from the Loire Valley, New Zealand, and South Africa focus on the grape's pure fruit flavors. However, Sauvignon Blanc has an alter ego and comes in one other style—oaked. In Bordeaux, a few hours south of the Loire Valley, it is blended with another white grape variety, Sémillon, and is fermented and/or aged classically in oak barrels. The oak increases the body of the wine and adds aromas of vanilla, nutmeg, and spice that generally those in the Fall category would prefer. The acidity, though, still remains refreshingly crisp.

In California, both oaked and unoaked styles of Sauvignon Blanc are made. Unoaked California Sauvignon Blancs do not have the pungency of those from New Zealand or South Africa. They do, however, have flavors of melon and fresh figs. Like other Sauvignon Blancs, they can have those green aromas.

So how can you tell if the style is likely to be richer and include oak flavors of vanilla, toast, and spice? Outside Pouilly-Fumé, if you see the words "Fumé Blanc" on the label, the wine has seen some oak. As mentioned earlier, Fumé means "smoked." However, "Fumé Blanc" has nothing to do with Pouilly-Fumé, which is the name of the appellation in the Loire Valley where an unoaked style is made. Robert Mondavi coined the marketing term "Fumé Blanc" to indicate the smoky character of the barrels in which he aged his oaked Sauvignon Blanc.

Another way to figure out whether a California Sauvignon Blanc sees any oak is to look at the back label. Many California back labels have a description of how the wine tastes. Sometimes they will come right out and say "oaky" flavor. However, you can also tell if you see taste descriptors such as "vanilla," "cream," "spice," or "toast." Those words mean that the wine has seen some oak. It also means it may be a style that appeals more to the Fall category than Spring.

CHÂTEAU DE SANCERRE, SANCERRE, FRANCE
Pale yellow color with aromas of citrus (lemon), steely minerality, and hint of fresh-cut grass. On the palate it is refreshing, dry, and light-bodied with bright, crisp acidity and a clean finish.

CRAGGY RANGE SAUVIGNON BLANC, MARTINBOROUGH, NEW ZEALAND
Pale yellow color with a slight green hue, intense aromas of citrus (lemon) with passion fruit aromas, and herbaceous green notes. On the palate it is dry and light-bodied, with a moderate length and a clean finish.

PINOT GRIGIO (PEE-no GREE-jee-o)

Pinot Grigio is one of the most popular wines in the United States. Why? It is dry, can be light- to medium-bodied, and medium acid to crisp, with aromas of pears and white peach and floral notes of honeysuckle.

The Pinot Grigio grape is the same grape as Pinot Gris, which you can read about in chapter 9. Pinot Gris in the French region of Alsace can get quite honeyed, unctuous, and rich, with spicy notes. However, the style this grape takes in Italy is much lighter, floral, and crisp, which Springs can appreciate.

Pinot Grigio in Italy predominantly grows in the northeast corner of the country with the most volume coming from the Veneto (the same region that Venice is in). There are also some very good-quality Pinot Grigios coming from the regions of Friuli and Alto Adige, where they become even more aromatic, light, and crisp. So keep a lookout for those place-names on the label.

In the United States, Italian Pinot Grigio is one of the top imported wines (if not the number one imported white wine). Ninety-five percent of Pinot Grigio–labeled wines come from Italy, and most of the other 5 percent comes from Australia and California. In California, acreage for plantings of Pinot Grigio grew 500 percent in the first decade of the new millennium.

In terms of taste profile, California and Australia Pinot Grigios have a more up-front, more obviously fruity style and tend to be less crisp than their Italian cousins.

Pinot Grigio is not a luxury wine known for long aging. Generally speaking it is at its best within the first three years of its vintage date, when its fresh fruit flavors are at their best. It does have a great reputation as a light, crisp aperitif or everyday wine that goes great with many light appetizers and dishes.

TIEFENBRUNNER

PINOT GRIGIO

———— 2011 ————

TIEFENBRUNNER PINOT GRIGIO, ALTO ADIGE, ITALY

Pale yellow color with ever so slight pale copper hue, soft white peach and floral aromas (honeysuckle, white flowers), and mineral notes. On the palate it is dry, fairly light-bodied with crisp, refreshing acidity that cleanses the palate.

ALBARIÑO (alba-REEN-yo) OR
ALVARINHO (alva-REEN-yo)

Albariño is another aromatic grape variety that Springs will very much appreciate. Its fruit flavors are solidly in the stone-fruit family (apricot, peaches, nectarines), with floral notes and a fresh vibrancy. It can also be quite delicate and refreshingly crisp.

Sounds a lot like Pinot Grigio, doesn't it? It does share some similar characteristics. Like Pinot Grigio, it is not known as a luxury, high-quality, over-$100 wine. However, Albariño can be a bit more aromatic, floral, and fresh, and generally has a higher level of acidity than Pinot Grigio.

Albariño comes from the Iberian Peninsula. In Spain it is called Albariño and in Portugal it is called Alvarinho. It's the same grape, just spelled differently.

Some U.S. wine regions are experimenting with Albariño, but as long as you know the grape's flavor profile, you won't be surprised by what's in the bottle.

DON OLEGARIO ALBARIÑO, RIAS BAIXAS, SPAIN
Pale straw yellow with perfumed aromas of refreshing citrus/lime, floral, white peach, grapefruit, and mineral notes. On the palate it is dry and bright, with fairly light body and crisp, clean finish.

GRÜNER VELTLINER (GROO-ner VELT-lean-er)

This Austrian white grape variety has become quite popular with sommeliers and increasingly popular with consumers. Unlike the grape varieties we have mentioned previously that appeal to Springs, Grüner Veltliner (or Grüner for short) is not as aromatic. It does, however, share some fresh Spring-like characteristics.

Grüner is dry, light-bodied, and has crisp acidity and can have modest alcohol (meaning under 12 percent). Its fruit characteristics are in the citrus family—grapefruit and lemon tones—but sometimes it has a honeydew melon or quince character. If you have never heard of quince before, it is related to apples and pears, and I find the flavor somewhere in between the two (see also Chenin Blanc on page 89). If you have never had one, go to a specialty market so you can add it to your "taste memory."

In terms of quality, Grüners run the gamut. You see them for less than $10, under screw cap, though there are some, which can age for a long time, that can go for more than $50.

One unique aromatic that Grüner is known for is white pepper. This does not mean the winemaker added white pepper to the wine; it is a characteristic of the grape itself. If you are unfamiliar with the aroma of white pepper, pick some up next time you go to the supermarket. White pepper comes up in other wines as well. It is a spice characteristic, but it is quite light and adds an additional fresh kick to the wine.

Grüner is also said to have aromas of lentils or celery. To be honest, though, I have never smelled this in Grüner; perhaps I don't eat enough lentils to recognize it.

Most Grüner comes from Austria with its most famous regions—Kamptal, Kremstal, and Wachau—in the Niederösterreich (NEED-er AH-ster-rike). You do see it in some other Eastern European countries, and it is being experimented with in the New World because of its popularity with wine geeks everywhere.

NIGL GRÜNER VELTLINER, KREMSTAL, AUSTRIA
Very pale color with watery rim, soft aromas of grapefruit, melon, honeydew, white flowers, hint of white pepper and minerals. Light-bodied, modest alcohol, and fairly delicate body with a refreshingly fruity finish.

WHITE RHÔNE—MARSANNE (MAR- san)/ ROUSSANNE (ROO-san)

These bosom buddy white grapes from the Rhône Valley, in France, create wines that are aromatic, delicately floral, and fruity with refreshing character. Right up any Spring's alley!

Marsanne is known for its citrus and stone-fruit (peach, apricot) characters, with floral notes of jasmine and acacia and honey. Roussanne is more fragrant, with notes of pear and herbal tea, and hints of honeysuckle. You generally see them blended together and rarely see these grape varieties bottled alone.

Marsanne dominates the white wines in the northern Rhône (Hermitage, Crozes-Hermitage, St.-Joseph; it is not allowed in Châteauneuf-du-Pape). Wines with a higher percentage of Roussanne are lighter and more fragrant, which Springs will enjoy even more.

Because these wines are associated with an area in France recognized for quality, they tend to be on the more expensive side (meaning generally over $20) and some can be over $150 (such as Jean-Louis Chave's Hermitage Blanc). Sometimes you see Marsanne/Roussanne oaked. If this is the case, they are more likely to be liked by a Fall than a Spring. The versions that Springs will like are the dry, delicate, unoaked, and crisp kind.

In the New World, Rhône-style whites are generally fruitier in style (and can sometimes be less expensive). Roussanne and Marsanne are grown in California, mainly by producers who are huge fans of Rhône Valley style. These producers have been dubbed the "Rhône Rangers." Australia is also experimenting with Marsanne and Roussanne.

DOMAINE DES CADASTRES ROUSSANNE, LANGUEDOC, FRANCE

Citrus fruit and white flowers on the nose. On the palate, it is dry and crisp with flavors of peach and apricot, and with lingering floral and mineral notes.

ROSÉ (row-ZAY)

Rosé is a style of wine that falls between white and red (in other words, pink). For those Springs who say they "only like white wine," rosés are a perfect gateway to reds. Rosés are made by letting the skins of red grapes soak in the freshly pressed juice for a few hours before fermentation begins. The color from the skins is extracted into the wine.

Rosés can be made from virtually any red grape variety. For example, Zinfandel is a red grape variety. In fact it's a variety that Winters may enjoy for its richness. However, when the grapes are pressed and sit on the skins for a only few hours, the juice becomes pink. When made this way it's called White Zinfandel.

The longer the juice sits on the skins, the more color the resulting wine has. The color range for rosés is quite wide, from ones that look like white wines with the faintest hint of pink to a pale, bright red.

Rosés can also be made by blending white wine and red wine together (e.g., rosé Champagne).

Why create a style like this? The skin contact imparts flavors that aren't usually found in white wines. We go from the lemon, grapefruit, and peach you see in white wines to more red-berry aromas—strawberry, cherry, raspberry, etc. And because the wine sits on the skins for only a few hours, the wine doesn't absorb much tannin (bitterness or astringency). So, Springs can get the benefit of the fruit flavor that the other seasons appreciate without any of the bitterness.

Rosés come in a variety of sweetness levels as well. They can be sweet, slightly sweet, off-dry, or dry. Springs vary in their sweetness preferences. There are some Springs who love their wines sweet and others who won't touch anything sweet. What they both appreciate, though, is wines that are fresh, clean, bright, and delicate. Though White Zinfandel is not technically a dessert wine, it is fairly sweet for a table wine. On the opposite end of the spectrum, rosés from the region of Provence, in southern France, are bone dry.

There are rosés made in the four corners of the world, but there are no regulations requiring wineries to disclose their wines' sweetness level. Therefore, it's always a good idea to ask the wine store staff or sommelier so that you get the level of sweetness you prefer.

BERINGER WHITE ZINFANDEL, CALIFORNIA
Pale pink with aromas of fresh strawberry, honeydew, and citrus. On the palate it is slightly sweet and easy drinking, with simple fruit flavors toward the finish.

CHÂTEAU MINUTY, CÔTES DE PROVENCE, FRANCE
Pale salmon pink color with aromas of ripe strawberry, watermelon, minerals, and spice. On the palate it is dry, fairly delicate with fresh acidity, nicely balanced, and a moderately long finish.

BEAUJOLAIS (BO-joh-lay)

Those in the Spring category are sensitive to bitterness. Since many red wines have tannin, you might not expect to see any reds in this chapter. However, if Beaujolais could be a white wine, it would be. It is light, soft, delicate, refreshing and fruity.

When I was still working and living in London, I had some French friends who took me on a picnic. We all went to the supermarket to pick up groceries. Being American, I went straight for the potato chips and soda. That's what we do! However, when I arrived, they laughed at me and taught me how to picnic French style. They had a large, long loaf of French bread, different types of cheese, some strawberries, and Beaujolais. This was before I knew anything about wine and I thought to myself, "Wow, how fancy shmancy!

They brought wine!" But to them, Beaujolais was a very casual picnic drink. It was the best picnic I've ever had. Now, every time I think of picnics, I think of Beaujolais.

Beaujolais is not the name of the grape. Beaujolais is a region in eastern France where the wine is made with a grape called Gamay. Gamay is known for wines with very low tannin, so low bitterness, with a fruity character and modest alcohol. It's neither as aromatic or as noble as Pinot Noir nor as acidic as Barbera. However, it is still fruity, fresh, light, and delicate. The perfect red for Springs.

You often hear that white wines should be chilled and red wines should be served at room temperature. However, Beaujolais Nouveau, Beaujolais, and Beaujolais-Villages are exceptions. These soft, delicate reds—with fruity raspberry flavors and moderately high acidity—become even more refreshing with a little chilling. (For more information on serving wine see chapter 13.)

There are a few styles of Beaujolais that you should be aware of. Beaujolais Nouveau is the softest, fruitiest, and most modest in alcohol and tannin. And although it is generally dry, it can also taste like candy. A step up is Beaujolais, then Beaujolais-Villages and finally Cru Beaujolais (where you will see the name of the village like Morgon or Moulin-à-Vent or Fleurie on the label).

Cru Beaujolais is the highest quality, the most complex, and the most expensive style of Beaujolais. In truth, these wines are never really very expensive; you rarely see a Cru Beaujolais over $40. This makes them an incredible value.

LOUIS JADOT BEAUJOLAIS, FRANCE

Clear, pale, ruby red color, with soft aromas of raspberries, cherries, and a hint of minerals. On the palate it is dry, with fresh acidity, soft tannins, and delicate structure. Simple, fruity, and enjoyable.

BARBERA (bar-BEAR-uh)

Now we are off to Italy. Barbera is a red grape found in the hilly region of Piedmont in Italy. "Piedmont" means "foot of the mountain" in Italian and indeed you can see the Alps from here.

Barbera is a great Spring wine because it has crisp, refreshing acidity, especially for a red. It is this "zing" that makes it pair well with many types of food. Acid makes the flavor of food "pop" and cleanses the tongue of any oil or fat, preparing you for the next bite.

The flavor profile is solidly in the cherry family; sometimes bing cherry and sometimes black cherry, but cherry nonetheless. The wine has some mineral aromas and sometimes it can have a fresh herbal characteristic, though more reminiscent of oregano or basil than the fresh-cut grass of Sauvignon Blanc or the green bell pepper found in Cabernet Sauvignon.

On some Italian wine labels (including Barbera) you will see the name of the grape plus the name of the area it comes from. For example, you may see Barbera d'Asti. This means that the grape used to make the wine is Barbera and it comes from the area of Asti. If you see Barbera d'Alba on the label, that means it is Barbera from the town of Alba. Prices of Barbera range from under $10 to over $30; it is rare to find a Barbera for more than $50. These are great value wines.

VIETTI BARBERA D'ASTI TRE VIGNE, PIEDMONT, ITALY
Medium ruby color with aromas of ripe cherry, mineral notes, and a hint of vanilla and spice. On the palate it is dry, with medium body, refreshing acidity, and soft, plush texture. Goes great with fresh salads, pizza, pork, and rotisserie chicken.

PINOT NOIR (PEE-no nwahr)

I have rarely seen a grape with such fanatics as Pinot Noir. People are crazy about this grape, and for good reason. Pinot Noir makes some of the finest wines in the world.

It is known for being very aromatic, sometimes referred to as perfumed. Its fruit aromas are reminiscent of the red berries (strawberries, cherries, raspberries) and also some lighter black fruits (blackberries).

Pinot Noir also has high acidity for a red grape. This gives it the freshness that Springs like, but it also gives it the ability to age for *decades*.

> Pinot Noir is known as "the headache" or "heartbreak" grape by those who grow it because it is so difficult to grow. It is also very sensitive to heat and to winemaking techniques. It's a fairly high maintenance grape. This is one of the reasons why the price for Pinot Noir, which starts at about $15, can go well over $1,000.

I consider Pinot Noir a "cusp" grape variety, which means it bridges Spring and Summer. This is because Pinot Noir can be made in a very fresh, crisp, delicate style that will appeal to Springs and it can be made boldly fruity with the more robust structure that Summers crave. This will depend on where it is grown and how it is made.

Like Riesling, Pinot Noir shows a "sense of place." This means it shows evidence of where it comes from in its flavor profile. People can taste the difference between Pinot Noir that was grown on different plots within the very same vineyard.

Burgundy, where it originated, is its classic region and that's where you see the highest quality and prices. You may not see the words "Pinot Noir" or "Burgundy" on the label, but you will see the word "Bourgogne" (Burgundy in French). If it says "Bourgogne" and it's a red wine, it's made with Pinot Noir. In Sancerre in the Loire Valley, it is even lighter in body and higher in acidity— very Spring-friendly. It also grows in Germany, where it is called Spätburgunder (SHBATE-ber-goon-der). In Italy, it is called Pinot Nero. Old World Pinot Noirs (meaning from Europe) generally have a more delicate structure, more crisp acidity, and more mineral notes than those of the New World (outside Europe).

Pinot Noir grows in a variety of places around the world, but it is not a "beach bunny" grape. It doesn't really do well in very warm or hot climates. Just as some people sunburn too easily at the beach, Pinot Noir is quite sensitive (thin skins).

Even in California, which is synonymous with sun and the beach, Pinot Noir is grown in the cooler climates—Santa Barbara, Sonoma, and Carneros to name a few. It also grows in the cool regions of Oregon, known for some high-quality Pinot Noirs. Other good areas for Pinot Noir are New Zealand, Tasmania, and Chile. Pinot Noirs from the New World tend to be a bit more up-front and obvious in their fruit.

JOSEPH DROUHIN LAFORÊT BOURGOGNE ROUGE, FRANCE

Clear, pale ruby color with aromas of fresh strawberries, cherries, and minerals. On the palate it is dry, with light body, fresh, crisp acidity, and soft structure.

SPRING PREFERENCE SUMMARY	SPRING RESPONSE TO A SOMMELIER:
CONCENTRATION: light	
TANNIN (BITTERNESS AND STRUCTURE): none to low	"I like my wines light-bodied with bright, crisp acidity. I like wines that are aromatic, floral, and delicate."
ALCOHOL TOLERANCE: light	
ACIDITY PREFERENCE: high	

PEACH

BERRIES

PEAR

BANANA

PINEAPPLE

PLUM

FRUITY

RASPBERRIES

STRAWBERRIES

SUMMER

S UMMER IS FUN IN THE SUN. Summer is the warmest and sunniest time of the year and this is when you see fruits in the supermarket that you don't see for the rest of the year—berries (strawberries, raspberries, blackberries, blueberries), stone fruit (cherries, peaches, nectarines, plums), and tropical fruits (pineapple, guava). Those in the Summer category prefer wines that are obvious in their ripe fruit character.

Your responses to the quiz suggest that you belong in the Summer category. Your answers generated a score in between Spring and Fall. You prefer wines that are a bit fruitier and richer than Spring, but not as rich or tannic as Fall.

Statements made by Summers that may correspond to your quiz answers:

» I take some cream and sugar in my coffee or tea
» I like milk chocolate
» I sometimes have lemon on my fish, and prefer orange juice

» I like my food mild to medium spicy

» I prefer medium-bodied wines

» I prefer sweet/candied scents

» I like bubble gum or fruity gum

» I snack on something light like a piece of fruit

Summers differ from Springs and Falls. They don't necessarily look for the crisp zing that Springs crave, and some wines that Falls (and definitely Winters) prefer can be too bitter or astringent for Summers' taste. If you find you are on the cusp of one of the other categories, explore the wines and see which ones you prefer. Have fun exploring!

WINES SUMMER MAY ENJOY

SOAVE (SWAH-vay)

Soave rhymes with "summer day"! Soave is a soft, fruity Italian white wine that Summers will enjoy.

Soave is not the name of the grape, but rather the name of the region it comes from in the northeastern region of the Veneto. Don't know where that is exactly? If you know where Venice is, go two hours west and you'll be sure to hit it.

The name of the white grape used to make Soave is Garganega (gar-GAH-negg-ah). Garganega's aromas can be quite fruity—in the citrus and apple family, leaning more toward Red Delicious apples than the crisp, acidic Granny Smith apples that Springs enjoy. It can also have a delicate almond flavor. Summers will appreciate this wine for its medium body and well-balanced acidity, meaning it's not too crisp or acidic and it has a soft texture.

TEDESCHI SOAVE CLASSICO
Straw yellow color with moderate aromas of pear, apple, almond, and a hint of flowers. On the palate it is medium-bodied, with a round mouthfeel with ripe fruit. It has moderate acidity and alcohol and a soft texture. Finishes clean.

CHENIN BLANC
(SHEN-in-BLONK)

Chenin Blanc is one of my favorite white grape varieties. Well, it is now. Back when I sat the Master of Wine exam for the first time, in 2006, it was my nemesis. I failed the exam that year because of this little white grape. Out of the thirty-six wines I had to identify blind, I misidentified three wines made with Chenin Blanc. Guess what I tasted for the next year before I took the exam again?

Summers will love Chenin Blanc for its fruit. It can taste of fresh apples, pears, and quince in some places, and be quite exotic and tropical in others. It is generally moderate—medium body, medium acidity, and medium alcohol. This is why Summers will appreciate Chenin Blanc. In the Loire Valley, where it originates, Chenin Blanc has a softness and an easygoing character.

CLASSICO

You will see wines labeled Soave and Soave Classico. "Classico" is a term you may see on other Italian wine bottles (e.g., Chianti Classico). When you see it on bottles of Italian wines, it means that the grapes used to make that wine come from a specified region from within the traditional, original boundaries of the region.

The original region of Soave was defined and limited to about 1,100 hectares (2,720 acres) in 1927. It then expanded several thousand acres with the creation of new rules in 1968. Soave Classico, however, refers to the original, historic area outlined in 1927.

What's the difference? It can definitely be argued that the Classico wines are of higher quality; the original boundaries were set for a reason and the wines demonstrate a sense of place (see chapter 7).

Chenin Blanc has been grown for over one thousand years in France's Loire Valley. It's in the Loire that it is known for its pear and quince aromas, and it can have some lovely floral aromas of acacia as well. You will see on the label names like Touraine, Anjou-Saumur, and Vouvray. Summers will prefer these wines to those from regions such as Savennières, where Chenin Blanc becomes more of what a Fall would enjoy—more baked pears (some say bruised apples) with hints of spice.

QUINCE

My first experience with quince was as a sweet brown jam to go with cheese after dinner. I didn't know it was a fruit that was like pears. Quince are golden yellow, have a pear shape, and the texture of the flesh is kind of a cross between a pear and hearty apple.

Chenin Blanc in Vouvray can be somewhat of a chameleon—it can be dry, sweet, sparkling, or still. Unfortunately it won't be clear by looking at the label. If you are confused, and to be sure you get one you like, ask the sommelier or retail staff at the store to clarify what style it is. Someone there tasted it, so they will know.

South Africa is now the world's largest producer of Chenin Blanc. Some producers there call it Steen. Regardless of what they call it, their Chenin Blanc takes on tropical fruit characters such as guava, bananas, and pineapple. Some Summers will love these exotic, tropical fruit flavors.

Chenin Blanc is also found in California, where it develops fruit characteristics in between those of the Loire and South Africa. You also see some oaked examples in California and they tend to be richer in style with some spice. These oaked styles will be more along the lines of what Falls would appreciate.

DOMAINE DE VAUFUGET VOUVRAY, LOIRE VALLEY, FRANCE
Pale straw yellow with slight greenish hue, moderate aromas of pear and quince, minerals, and slight wet wool. On the palate it has a hint of sweetness, a medium body, acidity, and alcohol. This is a very easygoing wine. It has finesse, with good balance and medium length.

FOOT OF AFRICA CHENIN BLANC, WESTERN CAPE, SOUTH AFRICA

Pale straw yellow color with slight green hue, moderate aromas of citrus, pear, hint of quince and tropical guava fruit on the palate. Medium body with fresh acidity and moderate alcohol. Well balanced, ripe fruit, medium length. Great value wine for Summers.

CHENIN BLANC
2011

SOUTH AFRICA

TORRONTÉS (tore-on-TEZ)

Torrontés is a very aromatic grape, with wonderful summer stone fruit, that Summers may love. Torrontés is the number one white grape variety grown in Argentina and is grown in the highest altitude vineyards in the world, near the Andes mountains.

Years ago I was at a trade tasting and just happened to be walking behind a chef who was also tasting. When we got to a table where a Torrontés was being poured, he looked pensive as if trying to analyze the wine. I asked him what he thought of it and he exclaimed, "Coriander! That's it! This smells just like coriander!" I'm not a chef, and I think I use the coriander in my spice rack once a year, if that, so I couldn't really relate. Later I bought a bottle of Torrontés and went to my spice rack. I smelled my small bottle of coriander, trying to register what it smelled like to me, and then tasted the wine. The chef was right. It does smell like coriander! Coriander has a light citrusy note and Torrontés smells a bit like it.

That could be a good tip for you. When someone says a wine tastes like coriander or nutmeg or cinnamon, test it out for yourself. I do it all the time! Like other methods I mention in chapter 3, this is a great way to train your nose to catch different aromas/flavors and to build your taste-memory portfolio.

If I tell you its perfume is quite floral and it has a hint of a spice you may think "Hey, hang on a minute. I thought Spring wines were floral and spicy wines were Fall. Why is this one a Summer?" One reason is that it doesn't exactly fit within Spring or Fall, it is somewhere in the middle.

Additionally, using the milk analogy, the weight of Torrontés is in the whole milk range, which places it in the Summer category. The wine is almost always appreciated for its youthful, fruity vibrancy, which Summers may also like. Having said that, Falls may like this Summer wine for its slight spicy character and Springs may enjoy its intense floral perfume. Sounds like a crowd-pleaser. If you have a mixed group, try it out!

MICHEL TORINO CUMA TORRONTÉS, CAFAYATE VALLEY, ARGENTINA
Sunshine yellow color with perfumed aromas of apricot, peach, notes of flowers, and slight citrusy spice (hint: coriander). Body is medium to heavy with a round texture, moderate acidity, and moderate alcohol. It is well balanced and finishes clean with an aftertaste of ripe fruit.

VIOGNIER (VEE-own-YAY)

What a great Summer grape. Unfortunately, its French name gives some Americans trouble, and as a result its sales have suffered. What a tragedy! A huge missed opportunity of deliciousness!

Viognier is very much a Summer grape, but like Torrontés, it has elements that are for Springs, Summers, and Falls. Viognier is quite perfumed, with intense aromatics of honeysuckle, jasmine, and other white flowers. On the other hand, it can attain richness and weight that firmly plant it in Fall. However, Viognier's aromas and flavors are pure summer stone fruits (apricot, peach, nectarine) that place this wine clearly in Summer.

In California you see Viognier in a range of styles from unoaked to some that are almost reminiscent of an oaked Chardonnay. How to tell? Here's a tip. If you read the tasting notes on the back label and it mentions any of the following words—oak, barrel, vanilla, toasty—chances are the wine has seen some oak in its winemaking. In other words, it might be more in the alignment toward Fall than Summer.

Another unique aspect of Viognier is that it can be medium to low acidity and can have moderate to high alcohol. This is why Springs may think it's a bit too much for them. It's more of a Marilyn Monroe to Spring's Audrey Hepburn.

Viognier has been in the Rhône Valley for a few thousand years. There are some interesting legends as to how it got there. Some say Roman legionaries traveling through planted it. Others say Emperor Marcus Aurelius Probus brought the vine to the Rhône in the third century.

The most famous region in the Rhône Valley for Viognier is Condrieu. Viognier from Condrieu can be a cusp wine, between Summer and Fall, depending on how much vanilla, toast, and spice it gets from the oak barrels it is fermented and/or matured in.

Summers should take note of the Languedoc region of France for Viognier; many wines from here are fruity, fresh, and vibrant with aromas of peach and apricot. A great go-to place for Summers.

This grape is a beach bunny and it loves the intense sunshine in the Rhône, southern France, California, and Australia.

THE ABC MOVEMENT

Back in the 1990s and early 2000s there was a trend in the trade called ABC, or "Anything But Chardonnay." This was a time when sommeliers and consumers were looking for a Chardonnay alternative, and so Viognier had a bit of hype. The problem with Viognier, however, is that it's not as easy to grow as Chardonnay and so it's not as easy to make an inexpensive one. Because it is more difficult to grow and make, this may explain why we don't see more wineries pulling up their Chardonnay vines for Viognier.

LAURENT MIQUEL NORD SUD VIOGNIER, LANGUEDOC, FRANCE

Straw yellow color with slight greenish hue and moderate aromas of jasmine, honeysuckle, pear, and apricot. On the palate it is medium-bodied, round with slight oily texture with moderate acidity and alcohol. It is well balanced with a clean, fruity, and lightly floral finish.

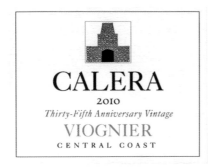

CALERA VIOGNIER, CENTRAL COAST, CALIFORNIA
Straw yellow color with moderate aromas of honeysuckle, white peach, and nectarine. On the palate it is medium-bodied with hints of custard flavors, moderate acidity, and slightly warm alcohol, finishing clean.

DOLCETTO (dole-CHET-oh)

Have you ever had the British dessert called summer pudding? I lived in London and during the summer many restaurants served it. When I finally ordered it, I was surprised. It's more like a soft, upside-down yellow cake from a bowl mold with a center of summer berries—cherries, raspberries, blackberries, boysenberries, blueberries—and the cake is entirely soaked in their juices. I mention this fruit dessert because when I tasted my first Dolcetto, it brought me right back to that first bite of British summer pudding.

Dolcetto comes from Piedmont, Italy. "Dolcetto" means "little sweet one" and it is a very appropriate description for this darling little red grape. The wine is dry, not sweet, but the impression of its berry fruits is sweet. Dolcetto doesn't have the celebrity status of the grape Nebbiolo, which makes the rich Winter wines of Barolo (see chapter 10) or the light cherry and high-acid wines of Barbera (see chapter 7), but it is a great find, especially for Summers.

Summers will enjoy its beautiful berry fruits and its medium everything—body, acid, and alcohol. It doesn't have Barbera's high acidity and it has soft tannins. Dolcetto doesn't register very high in bitterness, if at all, and it rarely sees much oak. This means less spice influence, although occasionally you will find some Dolcettos that have a soft, black licorice spice. This wine's primary flavor, however, is the summer berry fruit, and Summers may love it for that.

Dolcetto is not grown in very many places outside of Italy. However, you do see it in California in some places. The sunnier and warmer climate makes it a bit richer than its Italian cousin, and it is known for a bit more smoke and spice. So if you know a Fall, or you are on the cusp of being a Fall, you may really appreciate a this grape.

VIETTI DOLCETTO D'ALBA TRE VIGNE, PIEDMONT, ITALY
Medium ruby color with moderate aromas of black cherry, raspberry, blueberry, boysenberry, and mineral notes. On the palate it has a soft texture with moderate acidity and low tannins and alcohol, making it well balanced. Finishes clean with ripe summer fruits.

BONARDA (BOW-nar-da)

Bonarda is a black grape grown in Argentina, and there is a debate as to whether it is related to the grape variety so named in Piedmont or if it is Charbono in California. Confused yet? It actually gets worse, but I won't bore you with all the details.

Bonarda is the second-most-planted red grape variety in Argentina behind Malbec (see chapter 10). There are many times you see Bonarda blended with other grape varieties such as Malbec and Syrah.

On its own, however, Bonarda is on the medium side for reds and is quite fruity—red and black fruit flavors—with moderate acidity and modest tannins. Bonarda is a user-friendly, easygoing, fruity wine that Summers may enjoy, and it's generally a great value.

SUR DE LOS ANDES BONARDA, ARGENTINA
Medium ruby color with aromas of ripe red and black fruit—red cherry, black cherry, and blackberry. On the palate it is medium-bodied with up-front ripe fruit, moderate acidity, and soft tannins. It finishes clean with ripe berry flavors.

MONASTRELL (MONNA-strell)

This is one of my favorite Summer grapes. Monastrell is the Spanish name for Mourvèdre (more-VED-rah), which is a black grape that is often used in southern France for blending because it is rich, dark, and brooding. These characteristics are similar in Australia, where the grape is called Mataró, and in California, where it is usually called Mourvèdre.

However, south of Madrid it takes on a much more ripe, juicy, and fruity tone, particularly in the regions of Jumilla and Yecla on the east coast (roughly analogous to where the state of Georgia is in the United States).

The flavor is generally a mix of red fruits (cherry, raspberry) and black fruits (blackberry, boysenberry). These flavors are usually quite fresh, though they can sometimes lean toward stewed fruit, candied fruit, or jam.

What's interesting about Monastrell is that it can have a woodsy or toasty note and light structure, which makes you think it has been aged in oak even when it hasn't. That's just the flavors of the grape.

So if it has spice, why not put it in Fall? The grape in France, Australia, and California is more often than not used as part of a blend. In Spain it is bottled on its own, and there it has an intensely ripe juiciness and middle-of-the-road structure—medium body, medium acidity, and moderately soft tannin. Summers will appreciate this about the grape as they will its ripe, juicy red and black fruit flavors.

CASA CASTILLO MONASTRELL, JUMILLA, SPAIN

Medium deep ruby purple with aromas of juicy blackberry, plum, and black cherry with a hint of toast and minerals. On the palate it is medium-bodied with moderate acidity, ripe juicy flavors with soft tannins, and moderately long finish. Great value for Summers.

NERO D'AVOLA (near-oh DAV-oh-lah)

Both of my grandfathers are Italian. One grew up in Italy and then came over to the United States and the other was brought up in Queens, New York, with many relatives "off the boat." I'm not sure if they agreed on anything, except this: both their families were from the mainland of Italy and they were always suspicious of Sicilians. I've had each tell me on separate occasions that Sicily was nothing but the home of criminals and prisoners. The first time I brought home a boyfriend to meet the family, I was scared to tell them he was part Sicilian and part Polish. When I did, my grandfather said, "Polish I could forgive, but did he have to be part Sicilian?" I have a feeling it was somewhat tongue-in-cheek, but when this boyfriend and I did finally break up, he said, "I knew he wouldn't last. He was Sicilian."

My grandfathers would then probably scoff at my appreciation for this Sicilian black grape, Nero d'Avola, which has lasted much longer than that boyfriend.

Nero d'Avola is indigenous to Italy and is the most widely planted red grape variety in Sicily. It literally translates as "black of Avola." We see this often with Italian wine labeling. You see the name of the grape (in this case it's just its color) and a reference to the region. So Nero d'Avola really means "black grape from the commune of Avola."

The Nero d'Avola grape likes the sunshine and the warm temperature of Sicily, but unlike some other warm-climate grapes, it retains its bright, refreshing acidity. This makes it go very well with food. It has robust and ripe fruit flavors that are generally dark, meaning black fruit (blackberry), blue fruit (blueberry), and damson (plum). Summers may love this grape for its ripe and juicy fruit flavors.

In terms of tannins and bitterness, many examples I have tasted are fairly approachable and soft, especially those under $15. I have, however, seen some that are a bit more structured (which would be appealing if you are dining with Falls, as you both may enjoy it).

> *The Nero d'Avola grape likes the sunshine and the warm temperature of Sicily.*

Unfortunately, many Italian producers do not put tasting notes on the back of their labels, so look for words such as "rich tannins, structured, aging potential," which may indicate a wine that it is a bit heavier in tannins. Summers might find these a bit too bitter.

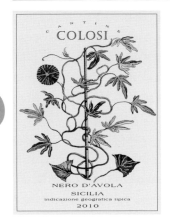

CANTINE COLOSI NERO D'AVOLA, SICILY, ITALY
Medium ruby color with aromas of very ripe black cherry and (odd as this may sound) cherry cola and minerals. It is medium-bodied with balanced moderate acidity, slightly warm alcohol, and fairly soft tannins. It is well balanced with a moderate finish.

CABERNET FRANC (CAB-er-nay FRONK)

Cabernet Franc originally comes from Bordeaux, where it is used as a blending grape with Cabernet Sauvignon and Merlot. Sometime in the seventeenth century, it was brought over to the Loire Valley (today only a few hours' drive north of Bordeaux) where it was allowed to stand on its own. The regions of Chinon and Bourgueil are particularly well known for high-quality Cabernet Franc in the Loire.

By itself, Cabernet Franc is known for red fruit aromas such as raspberry, but it also has a hint of black currant. When picked too early, or underripe, it can have a green element—leafy, but not green bell pepper like Cabernet Sauvignon. Some also say it has hints of violets.

On the palate it has a freshness, crisp acidity, medium body, and tannins which,

> You rarely see it as a dominant grape in Bordeaux, except in the case of Château Cheval Blanc, which has a stellar reputation. But Cheval Blanc is much richer and structured, more in the Fall or Winter camp.

though not very strong, do have a slight drying grip to them. This structure is what makes it go very well with food.

I traveled to France with a friend and we stopped to get a quick bite to eat in Chinon. It was fabulous to sit outside and grab some locally prepared charcuterie (which you can roughly translate as "deli meats," but that hardly does it justice). Looking at the tables around me, I noticed a lot of the locals and local vineyard workers having lunch. They had water glasses filled with Cabernet Franc from Chinon in front of them. So, of course, that's what I wanted. While there's a point to using great wine glasses, I fell in love with Chinon at that point because it was a place where I could be totally casual with wine—no fuss, no muss, just some good friends and wine.

Cab Franc is also grown in the New World (meaning outside of Europe), particularly in California, Australia, Chile, and South Africa. When grown in much warmer climates than the cool Loire Valley, however, the wines can take on a ripe, jam-like fruit flavor that Summers will also appreciate.

CHATEAU DU HUREAU LISAGATHE, PHILIPPE ET GEORGES VATAN, SAUMUR-CHAMPIGNY, LOIRE VALLEY, FRANCE

Medium ruby with aromas of raspberry, cherry, cranberry, and slight hint of tea leaves. On the palate it is medium-bodied with balanced crisp acidity, moderate alcohol and soft tannins. Very well balanced with moderately long length.

MERLOT (mer-LOW)

You've most likely heard of Merlot. It's a very popular grape. The name of this little black grape derives from the word for blackbird, or "merle," in French. Blackbirds are known to steal these little sweet black grapes throughout Bordeaux, France, where they originated.

According to the 2009 *Wine Handbook*, Merlot has been the second-most-popular red wine in the United States (behind Cabernet Sauvignon). Merlot is a crowd-pleaser and there is little wonder why.

Some have referred to Merlot as the "comfort food" of red wine. It has blackberry and dark plum fruit with medium body and soft, plush tannins (like falling into a pillow for your palate). Merlot also has a softer acidity than some grape varieties, including Cabernet Sauvignon. Its structure is one of the reasons why it is blended with Cabernet Sauvignon in Bordeaux. Merlot softens and takes the edges off the big, burly Cab. One of the words that comes up consistently in Merlot focus groups is "smooth." That describes Merlot well. This is an aspect that Summers really enjoy and why I place it in the Summer chapter.

You will also see Merlot mentioned in Winter (chapter 10). This is not a typo or a mistake. Merlot is one of the "cusp" grape varieties and makes different styles that will appeal to both of these seasons.

Merlot got a huge boost from some media attention in the 1991 *60 Minutes* show "The French Paradox," which proposed that red wine consumption decreases the incidence of cardiac disease. Given this, it probably won't surprise you to learn that after the show consumption of red wine skyrocketed 44 percent in the United States!

However, let's stick to what Summers like. Merlot is grown all around the world, from New York to New Zealand and, especially in warm climates, it gets quite juicy (blackberry, plum, but sometimes some raspberry, too). Many Merlots from Argentina, South Africa, Australia, New Zealand, and Chile are very fruity, soft, and approachable, perfect for Summers. California Merlots sometimes have a fruit jam note that Summers will love.

NOTE

Cusp wines can be good ones to order for large groups at a restaurant when you have a range of seasons. They can create a bridge between seasons and diverse style preferences.

FREI BROTHERS RESERVE MERLOT, DRY CREEK VALLEY, SONOMA, CALIFORNIA

Medium ruby with aromas of blackberry, black cherry, black plum, and a hint of vanilla. On the palate it is medium-bodied, with moderate acidity and balanced alcohol with a finish that reminds me of blackberry jam.

SUMMER PREFERENCE SUMMARY	SUMMER RESPONSE TO A SOMMELIER:
CONCENTRATION: medium	
TANNIN (BITTERNESS AND STRUCTURE): low to medium	"I like my wines obviously fruity, medium-bodied and soft-textured, without too much acid or tannin or alcohol."
ALCOHOL TOLERANCE: varies	
ACIDITY PREFERENCE: medium	

CINNAMON

DRIED FRUIT

LICORICE

ROSEMARY

ALMOND

CARAMEL

MUSHROOM

VANILLA

TOBACCO

FALL

L IVING IN THE AMERICAN NORTHEAST, I LOVE THE FALL SEASON. The
vibrant colors of the leaves, the weather turning a little crisp in the
morning, and of course holidays such as Halloween and Thanksgiving! Our appetites turn toward meals that are a bit richer and with
a hint of spice. I always think of hot apple cider, butternut squash, roast turkey
with chestnuts, sage stuffing, and pecan pie.

Your responses to the quiz suggest you are in the Fall category. This means
you generally prefer wines that are not too delicate, not too fruity or jammy,
yet not too strong either. Those in the Fall category prefer wines with similar
characteristics to this season—full of flavor and spice.

Statements made by Falls that may correspond to your quiz answers:

» I drink coffee with a little milk, generally no sugar
» I like both milk chocolate and dark chocolate, but really I
prefer semisweet chocolate—but that wasn't an option!

» I sometimes or never put lemon on my fish, and prefer orange or apple juice

» I definitely prefer medium spice and only occasionally nuclear

» I prefer "heavy cream" whites

» I prefer "whole milk" reds

» I prefer my perfumes spicy and I prefer cinnamon gum

» I prefer savory snacks

JAMMY

If you are not sure what "jammy" fruit smells like, go get some fresh strawberries and some strawberry jam or preserves. Cut up some fresh strawberries and smell them. Then open up the strawberry jam jar, stick your nose in there and take a large sniff. You will smell the difference. When you hear the term "jammy," it refers to the type of sweet, confected fruit you smell when you smell fruit jam.

Wines can take you to another time and place. We looked at an Enthusiast named Jim in chapter 1 who talked about how he was transported to Tuscany by drinking a Chianti Classico (a Fall wine). He felt the Tuscan sun on his face and smelled the oregano in the air.

I can definitely identify with this. The wines of Chianti Classico have an aromatic element of dried herbs and sometimes a savory meaty flavor. It reminds me somewhat of my grandmother's meat ragù sauce. It's practically a meal and a memory in a glass! Every time I taste one I am transported back.

WINES FALLS MAY ENJOY

CHARDONNAY (SHAR-duh-nay)

Chardonnay is one of the great noble white grape varieties. It is made in wine regions all around the world and found at practically every price point, from the modest to supreme luxury.

Chardonnay is generally known for an apple aroma, which can range from green Granny Smith to Red Delicious to baked. In cool climates it can even take on a citrusy note, and in warm climates the fruit is more tropical, like pineapple.

The only drawback to Chardonnay is that its aromas are subtle. It has fruit aromas, but they are not jumping out of the glass. In fact, if you did the Chest, Chin, Nose Test in chapter 4, you would probably find that you have to stick your nose in the glass with most Chardonnays to get their aromas. This is why you so often see oak influence (vanilla, spice, toast) to beef up the aromas.

Chardonnay comes from the region of Burgundy, in northern France. The easy thing to remember about Burgundy is that almost all white wines from Burgundy are made from Chardonnay grapes. Unfortunately, you won't see "Chardonnay" on most white Burgundy labels. European labels generally focus on the name of the region and not the grape variety.

While I was working in London, and way before I knew anything about wine, one morning I woke up and thought to myself, "What's all this talk about Chardonnay?" I had heard people at the office and at client dinners talking about it, saying things like "buttery" and "oaky." What did all that mean?

So after work I went to a wine store nearby named Oddbins. I walked up to the man behind the counter and said, "I want a fruity, buttery, and oaky Chardonnay" (without really knowing what I was talking about).

I also asked him, "How can you tell if it has oak in it?" and he said it will taste "oaky." Well, that didn't help me very much, but he did direct me to a specific Chardonnay.

So I ran home excited to try it. And it did taste fruity and buttery, and I tried to imagine what a piece of wood would taste like so I could really taste the oak. And you know something? It tasted even better than I'd imagined! Oak adds toasty, vanilla, and spice notes that I loved! For the first time, I felt like I was in the inner circle. I knew what "fruity, buttery, and oaky" meant. So Chardonnay will always have a special place in my heart.

The buttery notes in some Chardonnays come from a process during winemaking called malolactic fermentation. It turns the malic acid in wine (which is also the acid that makes green apples tart) to the lactic acid (the acid you find in milk) and creates a buttery flavor as a result. Chardonnays can also have a creamy texture on top of the buttery flavors. Falls will love these creamy textures and buttery flavors.

CHATEAU ST. JEAN SONOMA CHARDONNAY
Yellow gold color with aromas of ripe Red Delicious apples, vanilla, and nutmeg. On the palate it is fairly full-bodied with modest acidity, creamy texture, and slightly warm yet balanced alcohol. It has a moderate finish with lingering vanilla and cream flavors.

LOUIS JADOT MEURSAULT-CHARMES, PREMIER CRU
Pale yellow gold color with aromas of apples, minerals, hazelnuts, spice, slight toast, and a hint of vanilla. On the palate it is fairly full-bodied with balanced acidity and moderate alcohol. A rich wine with a long finish and many layers of complexity.

GEWÜRZTRAMINER (GUH-verz-tra-meen-er)

This grape has Fall written all over it. "Gewürz" in German means "spice" and its aromas and flavors will make Falls flip.

Though considered a white grape, the skin is actually pink. Sometimes this wine has a soft gold tone with a hint of pink (though it is far from a rosé or blush wine).

One flavor you will see written about Gewürztraminer is lychee fruit. Lychee is a tropical and subtropical fruit from China. We don't see a lot of them in everyday American cuisine, so they are a bit tough to describe if you have never had one. If you have never tasted a lychee before, check an Asian market or ask the next time you go to a Chinese restaurant. To me it's floral and perfumed, with a fruit character that I would describe as stone fruit (peach), though I have also heard it described as a blend of cherry and banana. Once you have a lychee, though, you will never forget the taste, and it mimics Gewürztraminer exactly.

Falls will also like the weight of these wines, which are generally full-bodied. They have a richer texture than most white wines, and Falls like this. They also tend to be low in acidity, which Springs would hate, but Falls don't mind at all.

Though it has German origins, the most famous Gewürztraminers come from Alsace, France. The grape is also grown in Austria and Italy, but in those countries the wines are a bit lighter than their more concentrated Alsatian cousins.

In the New World you see some very pretty Gewürztraminers from New Zealand and the United States (California and New York). They are more forward in their fruit than those from the Old World, but they still keep that spiciness and the more pronounced body that Falls will appreciate.

DOMAINE ZIND-HUMBRECHT GEWÜRZTRAMINER
Yellow gold color with intense aromas of lychee, honey, spice, and mineral. On the palate it is full-bodied and round with modest acidity, slightly warm alcohol, but very well balanced. It is fairly long with many layers of complex flavors.

PINOT GRIS (PEE-no GREE)

Pinot Gris is a white grape, but like Gewürztraminer, its skin is pink. It is also best known in Alsace, and shares some other characteristics. Pinot Gris can have some floral notes (orange blossom, acacia, honeysuckle). It is on the medium- to full-bodied side and also generally has medium to low acidity, depending on where in the world it is grown. Pinot Gris, too, has some spice, though to a lesser degree than Gewürztraminer. It is not as aromatic as Gewürztraminer and it has aromas of stone fruit (apricot, peach, and nectarine) more than lychee.

Some winemakers in Alsace produce Pinot Gris in a slightly sweet style, but outside of Alsace it is generally dry.

If you hear people say "Pinot Gris" it is not a short, cute nickname for Pinot Grigio (see chapter 7). Pinot Gris is the original name for the grape in France. In Italy it is called Pinot Grigio, but it's the same grape.

The name difference between Pinot Gris and Pinot Grigio has also come to represent a style difference. Outside of Italy, "Pinot Grigio" indicates a wine made in the Italian style—delicate, floral, and crisp (characteristics Springs like), while "Pinot Gris" tells you the wine is made in a style that leans toward the opposite end of the spectrum as in Alsace—floral, but rich fruit, honeyed and lightly spicy. The latter is the style that Falls will likely prefer. However, you do see styles that are somewhere in between, such as in Oregon and New Zealand, though the label will say "Pinot Gris."

WILLM PINOT GRIS VIN D'ALSACE, ALSACE, FRANCE
Straw yellow color with slight gold tone; aromas of apricot, honey, acacia flowers, and minerals. On the palate it has a touch of sweetness with a round, fairly full body with modest acidity and moderate alcohol. It is medium in length and finishes clean.

CARMÉNÈRE (CAR-men-air)

Carménère is Chile's flagship red grape variety. Falls will love this grape variety for its structure and its savory aromas. Believe it or not, Carménères have aromas that remind me of grilled meat and soy sauce.

Don't laugh! Wines can have savory aromas that make them taste almost like a meal in a glass. Don't get me wrong, they don't taste only of these flavors. Carménère does have rich fruit character (black cherry and blackberry). However, the savory aromas are unique to this grape and Falls will definitely pick up on them and appreciate them.

Carménère had a bit of an identity crisis in Chile. Carménère originally came from Bordeaux. However, Merlot and Carménère look very similar, and when the vines from Bordeaux were planted in Chile in the nineteenth century, it was very hard to tell the difference between them. Some of the vines they thought were Merlot were actually Carménère.

It was only in the mid-1990s that the two varieties were officially recognized as different in Chile, and varietal bottlings of Carménère have been permitted only since 1998. However, there are many bottles that say "blend of Merlot and Carménère," which might mean a field blend where it's uncertain how much they have of each!

It is a medium- to full-bodied grape depending on where and how it's grown and made. It is also known for modest acidity (which, again, doesn't bother Falls too much). Its tannins are there, making the wine almost chocolaty in texture. Summers might find some of the tannins in Carménère a bit bitter, yet Falls don't find them bitter at all.

Carmenère
D.O. Valle Central · Chile

TERRA ANDINA CARMÈNERE, CENTRAL VALLEY, CHILE
Medium ruby purple color with aromas of ripe blackberry fruit and black cherry, with elements of grilled meat and dried herbs. On the palate it is medium-plus-bodied with modest acidity, very fruity, with balanced medium acidity and moderate tannin. On the palate it has a medium finish with layers of complexity. Great value wine!

TEMPRANILLO (TEM-pra-NEE-yo)

Tempranillo is the most popular grape for high-quality wines in Spain, though you won't see the name on the label (remember, in Europe they focus on the name of the place it comes from). Ever hear of the wines from Rioja (ree-OH-ha)? They are made from Tempranillo.

Some have described it as Spain's answer to Cabernet Sauvignon, though it has nowhere near the dense structure and tannins that Cab has. Others have described it as a cross between Pinot Noir and Cabernet Sauvignon. I don't disagree with this. It has Pinot Noir's strawberry and red berry flavor, yet the color of Cab. Comparing it to grapes we know may help us understand it better, but Tempranillo should be appreciated for its own unique character.

Tempranillo's fruit can be red (strawberry, cherry, raspberry) and sometimes black (blackberry, boysenberry, mulberry). What Falls will appreciate is the savory character, similar to Carménère's grilled-meat aroma. It also has what I call a "bramble" note. This is a woodsy, earthy character that reminds me of the smells you get when walking through a forest in October or November. This adds complexity and layers of flavors that Falls will appreciate.

Tempranillo is grown all over Spain and you see medium-bodied versions, such as those from Navarre and La Mancha, and ones that are more full-bodied, richer, more tannic—Ribera del Duero and Toro.

Tempranillo also grows in Portugal. In the Douro Valley it is called Tinta Roriz (TEEN-ta HOR-eesh) and in the Alentejo (ALAN-tay-joo) region it is called Aragonez (ARA-gon-esh). Though differently named, they are all the same grape as Tempranillo. In fact, in Spain Tempranillo has many names—Tinto Fino, Cencibel, Tinto del País, and Ull de Llebre.

SPANISH WINE LABEL TERMS

On bottles of Rioja, you will see the following terms that refer to how long the wine has been aged.

"Joven" means young, and these wines generally do not see any aging in oak barrels. Summers will likely appreciate these wines more than Falls.

"Crianza" means the wine sees at least one year in oak barrels, though outside the region of Rioja, in the rest of Spain, it means that the wine has been in oak barrels at least six months.

"Reserva" is one year in oak, but it may not be released until its fourth year following the harvest.

"Gran Reserva" requires two years minimum in oak and may not leave the winery until its sixth year following the harvest.

Why should you care about this? As wine ages, it changes. The longer the wine ages, the more the aromas and flavors will go from fruit-focused to more savory, spicy, and earthy, which Falls will appreciate. The structure, too, will go from firm and sometimes slightly astringent to soft, plush, and harmonious. All of these things will appeal to Falls.

You may also see it blended with other grape varieties such as Grenache, Syrah, Cabernet Sauvignon, and Merlot.

This is an up-and-coming variety for the New World and you do see Tempranillo in California and Australia. So far they have not reached the quality levels you see in Rioja and Ribera del Duero, but they are great values and the quality is getting better each year.

PESQUERA RIBERA DEL DUERO, SPAIN
Medium ruby color with moderate aromas of dark fruits (blackberry, plum) with a hint of bramble and smoke. On the palate, however, it has mouth-filling fruit that is juicy with medium body, medium acidity, and balanced alcohol. The tannins are soft, fine, and supple; it has moderately long length that finishes with Fall-like spice.

SANGIOVESE (SAN-jee-o-VAY-zay)/ CHIANTI (key-ON-TEE)

Sangiovese makes one of the most popular red wines in the world: Chianti. In fact, Wine Intelligence, a leading wine research firm, did a study in 2007 and Chianti was the most recognized wine name behind Bordeaux and Champagne. However, some people still associate Chianti with the stereotypical round-bottomed bottle in a little wicker basket with a candle in it. It's so much more than that!

Sangiovese bursts with cherry fruit, but it can also have some dried cherry, which Falls can appreciate. It also has what I describe as a tomato sauce–like savory quality. It doesn't taste like tomato sauce, but it has an aroma reminiscent of the dried herbs and spices that you find in tomato sauces (oregano, for example). It can also have a certain "meaty" flavor that may remind you of a slow-cooked meat ragù.

One of the great hallmarks of Sangiovese, though, is its high acidity. It is this high acidity that makes food flavors pop, making some great food and wine pairings.

Sangiovese is grown all over Italy, though Tuscany is its true home. Like Tempranillo, it can be medium-bodied in some areas and more full-bodied in others. Here are some wines made with Sangiovese, listed in increasing weight and richness:

» Vino Nobile di Montepulciano (VEE-no no-BEE-lay dee MON-te-pull-chee-AH-no)
» Chianti (key-ON-TEE)
» Chianti Classico (key-ON TEE CLASS-ee-koh)
» Brunello di Montalcino (broo-NELL-oh dee mon-tal-CHEE-no)
» Super Tuscans

The Chianti region is roughly between Siena and Florence, in the center of Tuscany. You will also see "Chianti Classico" on some labels. In chapter 8 we noted that Classico is a term that refers to the original borders of the region before it expanded. Why do we care? Well, most Chianti Classicos are higher in quality than basic Chianti, which is also why they are a little more expensive.

You may also see the word "riserva" on the label. In Chianti, this means that the wine has spent more time aging in barrels. However, "riserva" doesn't necessarily mean higher quality. It just means that it may have more spice flavors.

Sangiovese is also grown in California, Australia and Argentina. In those countries it is generally riper and more obvious in its cherry fruit character than in Italy, and outside of Italy it is often blended with other grape varieties such as Syrah, Cabernet Sauvignon, and Merlot. In Tuscany, Super Tuscans are those made with certain French grape varieties (see chapter 10).

BARONE RICASOLI BROLIO, CHIANTI CLASSICO, ITALY
Medium pale ruby color with aromas of ripe cherry, raspberry, and a hint of dried cherry with something savory (herbs and grilled meat) and a hint of vanilla and toast. On the palate it is medium-bodied with fresh acidity, slightly warm alcohol, and moderate tannins. It is well balanced and has a moderately long finish that lingers with flavors of cherry.

PINOTAGE (PEE-no-TAHJ)

Pinotage is the flagship red grape variety of South Africa. Falls will appreciate its spicy tones and earthy character. It is also known for a particular aroma— I call it ash, but others refer to is as strong minerality. This probably sounds quite tame after the cat's pee in Sauvignon Blanc and the diesel in Riesling. Again, these aromas sometimes add complexity to the wine, making them more interesting.

We've spoken about Old World wines (European) and New World wines (everyplace else). South African wines are unique in that they have characteristics that bridge the two styles. They have the obvious, up-front fruit ripeness of the New World while holding on to some Old World reserve and complexity.

There are also Pinotages that fall into the "coffee camp," which means they have aromas of coffee, mocha, or coffee beans. Falls usually like these earthy and spicy aromas.

Pinotage has some very ripe red-and black-fruit aromas and healthy acidity, which makes it go well with food. It generally has medium body with moderate to sometimes more aggressive tannins. Falls can appreciate this structure.

Pinotage is grown all over South Africa, but some of the higher-quality Pinotages come from the region of Stellenbosch. It is also blended with other varieties, such as Syrah, Cabernet Sauvignon, and Merlot, for "Cape Blends." These can be good-value wines, and the Pinotage adds a touch of spice that Falls will like.

> *Pinotage has some very ripe red-and black-fruit aromas and healthy acidity, which makes it go well with food. It generally has medium body with moderate to sometimes more aggressive tannins. Falls can appreciate this structure.*

BEYERSKLOOF RESERVE PINOTAGE, STELLENBOSCH, SOUTH AFRICA

Medium ruby purple color with aromas of fresh, ripe raspberries and cranberries and hints of mulberries and blueberries, some vanilla, toast, and coffee, and strong mineral notes. On the palate it is medium-bodied with balanced acidity and moderate alcohol and moderate tannins. It is well balanced with nice length and finishes with red fruit flavors.

SYRAH (sir-AH)/SHIRAZ (sher-AZ)

You've probably heard of Syrah and Shiraz. Did you know they are exactly the same red grape? Syrah is its original name in France. Shiraz is what they call Syrah in Australia.

Syrah can have rich, jam-like fruit, particularly raspberry, but sometimes also blackberry and cherry juice. Summers may like Syrah for those reasons, and I consider it a cusp grape.

However, Falls will love Syrah because it has an element of spice—black pepper—that runs through most wines made from the grape. Depending on where it's grown it can also take on dried herb and earthy complexities that Falls will appreciate.

Falls will also like the weight of this wine, which can be medium- to full-bodied. Its tannins never quite get to the level of Cabernet Sauvignon, Nebbiolo, or Tannat, but they are definitely there.

Syrah comes from the Rhône Valley in southern France. It is the grape of the northern Rhône in particular and its most famous vineyards include Côte-Rôtie, Hermitage, Crozes-Hermitage, St.-Joseph, and Cornas.

Interestingly, this grape's origin has many legends. One speaks of its being planted by St. Patrick on the hill of Hermitage, in the Rhône Valley, in France. Another one speaks of its origins in the Middle East, in ancient Persia, with the hypothesis that it was named after the city of Shiraz.

> Syrah shows a "sense of place" (see chapter 7), and in the northern Rhône its environment has a huge impact on its flavors. Many flowers, plants, and herbs grow in southern France—olive trees, rosemary, lavender, thyme, and white cistus—and their aromas and flavors somehow find their way into the wine (though scientists are still baffled as to exactly how). Falls will love some of these layers of complex flavors in northern Rhône Syrahs.

Though the same grape, Australian Shiraz has much more obvious fruit and demands to be noticed. It can be fresh, but it can also be quite "jammy."

Similar to Pinot Gris and Pinot Grigio, the name difference between Syrah and Shiraz has also come to represent a stylistic difference. For example, Syrah is grown in Portugal and the ones that I have tasted that have "Syrah" on the label have more in common with northern Rhône (ripe fruit, but spice and herbs) than with Australia. We would then say this Portuguese wine is in a "Syrah" style (versus the plump, jammy, rich "Shiraz" style).

The grape is also grown in California, New Zealand, South Africa, Argentina, and Chile in the New World. However, in these places you are just as likely to see "Syrah" as "Shiraz" on the label. Those that are more restrained in their fruit and have more of an herbal character we say are in a "Syrah" style. Those that are jammy, with sweet fruit and black pepper notes, are said to be in a "Shiraz" style. This knowledge can help you in a restaurant if you want to choose one style over the other.

GUIGAL CROZES-HERMITAGE, RHÔNE VALLEY, FRANCE

Medium deep ruby color with aromas of very ripe dark fruit (blackberry, boysenberry, black cherry), spice (black pepper), dried herbs (rosemary), and minerals. On the palate it is medium-bodied with balanced acidity, moderate tannin and moderate alcohol. It has a moderately long finish with lingering notes of herbs and spice.

MOLLYDOOKER THE BOXER SHIRAZ, SOUTH AUSTRALIA, AUSTRALIA

Deep ruby and slightly opaque color with intense aromas of raspberry, cherry, black pepper, and hints of eucalyptus (and cherry Coke. What can I say? That's what I get!). It also has some sweet vanilla and slight coconut aromas. On the palate it has medium plus body with balanced acidity, warm alcohol (16 percent) and moderate tannins. It has moderate length and finishes with strong fruit and spice.

GRENACHE (gruh-NASH)/ GARNACHA (gar-NOTCH-ah)

Grenache (as it is known in France) is known for a ripe cherry flavor, but it also has elements of spice such as ginger, gingerbread, coffee, and other brown spices. There can be some black licorice spice and some black pepper, too, but it's generally not as pronounced as in Syrah. Falls will appreciate these layers of spices and flavors.

Grenache is another "beach bunny" grape that thrives in warm/hot environments. Heat and sun give Grenache very ripe fruit flavors, and it can get quite high in alcohol as well. This is OK by Falls. They can take the heat.

In the southern Rhône Valley, the most famous regions for Grenache are Châteauneuf-du-Pape, Gigondas, and Côtes du Rhône. Like Syrah in the northern Rhône, Grenache in the southern Rhône takes on the flavors of its surroundings. "Garrigues" is the term used to describe the shrubbery and vegetation in the surrounding area (as I mentioned in northern Rhône—olive trees, rosemary, lavender, thyme, and white cistus). "Garrigues" is also the term used to describe the earthy and herbal notes in the wine. Falls will really appreciate this garrigues character.

One of my benchmark aromas for Grenache is black licorice. I get this more in Spain, though, where they call the grape "Garnacha." Garnacha is grown all over Spain, but its most famous areas are Priorat and Calatayud.

In the New World, you see Grenache doing very well in Australia. There it is generally blended with Syrah and a black grape called Mourvèdre (same as Monastrell, see chapter 8) and in the trade we call these GSMs (or Grenache, Syrah, Mourvèdre blends). They have rich, ripe, obvious fruit with a hint of eucalyptus and can be quite jammy in their flavors.

ONIX PRIORAT, SPAIN

Deep ruby purple and opaque (almost inky) with aromas of very ripe black fruit (blackberry, plum), dried fig, and sweet vanilla with notes of rosemary, bramble, mint, and licorice. On the palate it is opulent and rich with modest acidity, fairly strong tannic grip, and warm alcohol. It has a long finish with many layers of complexity.

ZINFANDEL (ZIN-fan-dell)

Zinfandel is a black grape, though you do see it made into a sweet blush wine called White Zinfandel (see chapter 7). It's a European grape variety (Vitis Vinifera), but because it is predominantly grown in California, many consider it American. Zinfandel can make wines at every quality and price point, from the modest to the luxury level.

Zinfandel is made in many different styles, but it does generally have a nice level of acidity that makes it good to pair with some foods (such as pasta carbonara). The grape variety itself is an uneven ripener (meaning while some grapes in the cluster/bunch are ripe, others are green). When winemakers wait for all the grapes on the cluster to ripen, some of the grapes shrivel. These clusters have a higher concentration of sugar—so the potential alcohol in the wine is also higher—but this dehydration also adds a nice spice and light dried-fruit note. This makes it perfect for Falls.

The fruit character of Zinfandel can range from ripe cranberries to black cherry and even prune, depending on where it is grown. Falls will love that Zinfandels also have spicy notes, reminiscent of clove and cinnamon, and can have a chocolaty texture.

On the palate they can be medium-bodied and bright with light cherry fruit and they can be inky dark, with rich fruit and alcohol that can get up to 17 percent (this dips into Winter's territory; see chapter 10). If you are in the Fall category and you are sensitive to alcohol, you might look at the alcohol level when considering a Zinfandel.

You may hear that Zinfandel is the same grape as Primitivo (PREE-ma-TEE-voh). That's not exactly true. DNA profiling has found that both Primitivo and Zinfandel share common links to an ancient Croatian grape variety. In terms of characteristics, however, Primitivo shares many traits with Zinfandel. So if you are in an Italian restaurant and you are itching for a red Zinfandel and you don't see one on the wine list, go for a Primitivo!

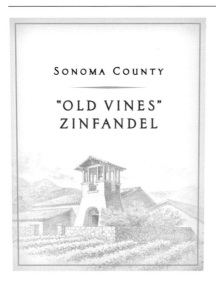

SONOMA COUNTY

"OLD VINES"
ZINFANDEL

ST. FRANCIS OLD VINES ZINFANDEL, SONOMA COUNTY, CALIFORNIA
Medium deep ruby with aromas of black cherry, cranberry, brown spice, toasted coconut, and vanilla. On the palate it is medium-bodied with balanced acidity, moderate tannins, and slightly warm alcohol. It has moderate length with a clean finish of cherry fruit and vanilla.

CONCENTRATION: medium to medium high

TANNIN (BITTERNESS AND STRUCTURE): medium to medium high

ALCOHOL TOLERANCE: medium to medium high

ACIDITY PREFERENCE: varies

"I like my wines medium- to fairly full-bodied with rich fruit yet with an element of spice, but not too tannic or high in alcohol."

119

BREAD

BLUEBERRIES

EUCALYPTUS

CHOCOLATE

TOBACCO

CARAMEL

COCONUT

BLACKBERRIES

COFFEE

WINTER

J UST AS THE SEASON OF WINTER makes us bundle up and seek out richer, heartier meals, those in the Winter category trend toward bigger, fuller-bodied, and higher-octane wines. Winters' wines put "meat on your bones" or "hair on your chest" (as my father would say about my mother's rich beef stew).

The human tongue can perceive only five basic tastes: sweet, sour, bitter, salt, and umami (see chapter 3). Wine generally has only the first three. The reason you fall into the Winter category is that your quiz answers suggest you can handle and prefer a higher level of bitterness and alcohol than the other seasons.

Statements made by Winters that may correspond to your quiz answers:

- » I take my coffee black, no sugar, no milk
- » I love spicy food (the hotter the better!)
- » I like any dark chocolate. It's not bitter to me!

- » If a wine's texture is analogous to heavy cream, I prefer that to whole milk or skim milk in my wines
- » I like rich, spicy, heady perfumes or colognes
- » I prefer spicy gums (like cinnamon) over bubble gum or mint
- » Candy bars or chocolate is my favorite snack

Winters' palates are less delicate then those of other seasons. If you are a Winter, you are likely a meat and potatoes kind of person (or osso buco and truffled mashed potatoes, whatever the case may be). Using the milk analogy, you prefer the texture of heavy cream to Springs' skim milk.

One possible explanation for Winters' preferences is that they have fewer taste receptors than the average person. This might explain why they need a wine that is intense in order to sense and appreciate it. Or they might just like intensity. The other seasons, particularly Spring, find the wines a Winter would like too strong, bitter, and alcoholic. However, a Winter would find the delicate, floral, light wines of spring lacking in flavor, diluted, and watery.

WINES WINTERS MAY ENJOY

CABERNET SAUVIGNON
(CAB-er-nay SAW-veen-yon)

Cabernet Sauvignon (aka "Cab") is a thick-skinned, red grape that makes rich, full-bodied wines with a high level of tannin or bitterness (see chapter 3). The fruit flavor profile for Cab includes black fruits (black currants, black-berries, plums).

While we don't see too many black currants on menus in the United States, British supermarkets have black-currant juice boxes called Ribena for kids.

A NOTE ON AGING

When I met my husband, he knew only two things about wine: the brand name Robert Mondavi and the philosophy of "the older the better." Because of their intense tannins and lush fruit (and generally good acidity), Cabs from the best regions can age for longer than other grape varieties. However, know that as wine ages, its fruitiness diminishes, the tannins soften, and the aromas turn more earthy and spicy. In other words, they turn into wines that appeal more to the Fall category. Therefore, if you are a Winter who really likes your wines with luscious fruit, strong structure, and some "punch," drink them younger.

When I started learning about wine and people mentioned black currants, I went to the supermarket and bought some to taste. Ribena Blackcurrant Drink (or concentrate) isn't widely distributed in the United States, but you might find black currants in your supermarket or perhaps a specialty grocery store.

You will also hear people talk about "cassis" aromas and flavors when talking about Cabernet Sauvignon. Cassis is black-currant liqueur. This may be easier to find, but the flavor is obviously a bit different than fresh black currants.

Cab has a strong tannic structure. These tannins will taste very dry, bitter, and astringent to a Spring, but Winters don't mind this at all. However, these tannins are the reason Cabs can age for a long time. They provide the structure for them to stand the test of time.

Cab can stand up and be complemented by great amounts of new oak (remember, oak provides flavors of vanilla, coconut, cedar, tobacco).

It is the buxom beauty of the lot, and it has a lot of admirers. That's why Cab can be found in every market, wine store, and restaurant at quality levels ranging from modest box wines to the most prized collectors' "cult" wines.

California Cabs take on a super-ripe richness because of that warm and intense California sunshine. Cab is grown all over California and at every price point. Napa Valley Cabs tends to be the most famous (and expensive) and they are the darling of steak houses everywhere, for a good reason. You can't go wrong with a Napa Cab and a big hunk of beef.

Bordeaux is the original and classic home of Cab. These wines may be less showy in their ripe fruit than those grown in California, but they can be quite voluptuous yet refined. Careful though: if it says only "Bordeaux" on the label (with no more specific region labeled), it is probably mostly Merlot, which is less structured and softer than Cab.

Bordeaux is where Cab shows the most "sense of place" (see chapter 7). That is, it shows the influence of where it is grown. The Pauillac region of Bordeaux, for example, is known for producing wines that are quite powerful and masculine in their tannic grip, with aromas of lead pencil and cedar, while the Cab-based blends in Margaux (we're still in Bordeaux) have a powerful structure but are a bit more rounded and feminine, with soft aromas of violets.

CULT WINE

You will hear the term "cult wine" when talking about some California wines that are made in small quantities by high-end wine producers who charge just as much as, if not more than, first-growth Bordeaux. Typically you will find California cult wines in the Napa Valley, but not exclusively. Some of the more famous cult Cab brands are Araujo, Bryant Family, Colgin, Dalla Valle Maya, Grace Family, Harlan Estate, Moraga, Screaming Eagle, and Vineyard 29. To give you an idea of the prices of some of these, a bottle of 1997 Screaming Eagle was recently sold at just under $4,000, whereas a bottle of Château Lafite Rothschild 2000 (great vintage) was sold for a little over $2,700.

In 1976 Steven Spurrier, a British wine merchant, hosted a wine competition in France. The judges included some of the best known palates of the day. They tasted the wines blind, meaning the names of the wines were kept from the judges. They sipped, slurped, and critiqued the wines with much meticulousness and integrity. What were the winning wines? Two Napa Valley wines— the Stags' Leap Cabernet Sauvignon and the Chateau Montelena Chardonnay. This event became known as the Judgment of Paris, and it put California on the map for high-end luxury wines that can rival the classics of France.

You also see Cabernet Sauvignon in Italy, where it is used to make so-called Super Tuscan wines.

Super Tuscans

Some producers in Tuscany wanted to create a style of wine so high in quality that it would rival top-growth Bordeaux. To do this they wanted to include Bordeaux varieties.

For example, in the 1940s Mario Incisa della Rocchetta planted Cabernet Sauvignon and Cabernet Franc on a tiny plot of land next to his castle as a hobby, and called the wine made from this plot Sassicaia or "place of many stones" in Italian. This wine is 90 percent Cabernet Sauvignon and 10 percent Cabernet Franc. Years later, but within the same noble family, the Marchese Piero Antinori created wines with Cabernet Sauvignon and Cabernet Franc, along with some Sangiovese (see chapter 9) and aged them in small French oak barrels. These wines are of very high quality and today are luxury status wines.

The problem was that the laws were quite strict and would not allow these "foreign" grape varieties to be included in wines labeled with the high-quality regional stamp. So, these two producers thumbed their noses at the laws and made them anyway. The government classified these two wines as mere "table wine" despite their obvious high quality.

This caused quite a revolution, and thus was born a new name: Super Tuscan. You won't see the phrase "Super Tuscan" on the label, but these wines truly put Italy on the international scene for high-quality, modern-style wines.

You may see wines at a lower price point than luxury (meaning below $25) that try to call themselves Super Tuscans, but these are more like "baby Super Tuscans." The term "Super Tuscan" is really reserved for only those really high-quality wines over $50 that have Cabernet Sauvignon and Merlot in the mix.

Note that Super Tuscans made with more Sangiovese will appeal to Falls, while those made with predominantly Cabernet Sauvignon will likely be more agreeable to those on the cusp of or in the Winter Category.

You see Cabernet Sauvignon in pretty much every wine country in the New World—Argentina, Australia, New Zealand, South Africa, and all over the United States. Chile makes some very ripe, rich Cabs, too, and they are great values. Chilean Cabs also often have flavors of savory herbs that Winters (and some Falls) may really enjoy.

CHÂTEAU HAUT-BATAILLEY, PAUILLAC, BORDEAUX, FRANCE

Medium ruby purple color, slightly opaque, with aromas of black currant, mineral notes, toast, cedar, and hint of coffee. On the palate it is full-bodied and round, with balanced acidity, firm tannic grip, dense chocolaty texture and moderate alcohol. It has a very long finish with many layers of complex flavors and is extremely well balanced.

PINE RIDGE FORTIS CABERNET SAUVIGNON BLEND, NAPA VALLEY, CALIFORNIA

Medium deep ruby purple with aromas of very ripe black currant and cassis with notes of eucalyptus, vanilla, and toast. On the palate it is fairly full-bodied with moderate acidity, slightly warm alcohol, and well balanced, firm tannins. Moderately long finish with complex notes that linger to the finish.

TANNAT (tan-NOT)

If you haven't heard of this black grape, don't worry. Most people in the wine industry haven't, either! It's a powerhouse of a grape: a big boy. Just how big? To give you an idea, in France Cab is used to soften it!

Known for rich blackberry fruit, Tannat has some of the strongest tannins (besides Nebbiolo). That is likely how it got its name (from tannins to Tannat, get the connection?). Winters, however, can look past that tough-guy exterior and get its blackberry appeal. Tannat has a deep rich color and structure that can handle a fair amount of oak. That means you can get Tannats that have lots of the flavors associated with oak (vanilla, toast, spice). Winters will appreciate these flavors on top of the rich black fruit.

Tannat generally comes from one of two places. The first, and the place of its classic origins, is the Southwest appellation of Madiran in France.

The second region is Uruguay. Yes, you read right. The sunshine in Uruguay ripens these grapes enough to tame those incredibly intense tannins and make wines that are luscious and obviously fruity. This is an emerging wine region and not only can you get great deals now, but the wines are getting better and better with each passing vintage.

VIÑEDO DE LOS VIENTOS TANNAT, ATLÁNTIDA, URUGUAY

Deep and opaque ruby color with aromas of blackberry jam, blackberry syrup, and cassis with a slight bramble-and-cigar note that adds complexity. On the palate it is fairly full-bodied with warm alcohol and firm tannic grip. Definitely a Winter wine.

NEBBIOLO (neb-BEE-o-lo)

This classic Italian red grape from Piedmont makes the wines of Barolo and Barbaresco. It is also quite powerful, but unlike other grapes in its fighting class, it is highly aromatic and quite acidic. It is known for red fruit aromas (cherry, raspberry) with floral (rose petals, violet) and herbal notes (tea leaves) yet it has powerfully strong tannins and is fairly high in alcohol. Think of a buff Gerard Butler in the movie *300*, but in a tux with a splash of cologne and holding a bouquet of roses. That sums up Nebbiolo.

Deep color = more powerful wine? It can, but not necessarily. Cabernet Sauvignon and Tannat are grape varieties that are rich in tannin and color pigmentation (both of which are related to the same family of chemicals called phenols). Generally speaking, when a grape is rich in one, it is rich in the other. You can probably make the guess that if the wine is deep in color, likely it will be a powerfully tannic wine. However, Nebbiolo can be fairly pale, especially versus these other heavyweights, and yet it has one of the most powerfully tannic structures of most red grapes. So deep color doesn't always mean more powerful weight and structure.

Nebbiolo lives and thrives in Piedmont, Italy, for the most part. The masculine Barolo and his softer, more fragrant sister, Barbaresco, are the best-known and highest-quality regions for Nebbiolo. Again, for many European labels, the place the wine is from will be listed on the label instead of the grape that is used. For wines made from Nebbiolo, look for labels that say Barolo, Barbaresco, Langhe, or Gattinara.

You do also see Nebbiolo in Australia and the United States. They do not have the structure and aging ability of their Italian cousins, but you do see more experimentation with this grape in the New World.

PIO CESARE BAROLO, PIEDMONT, ITALY

Medium ruby color with perfumed aromas of cherry and strawberry fruit with notes of tea leaves, rose petals, and hints of minerals. On the palate it is full-bodied with crisp yet balanced acidity, powerful tannins, and slightly warm alcohol. Despite its intensity, it is very well balanced, quite seamless with many layers of complexity, and has a long finish.

MALBEC (MALL-beck)

Winters will really appreciate the wine from this little black grape. Similar to Tannat, Malbec's mother tongue is French, but it has made huge strides in South America (particularly Argentina). A decade ago no one was talking about Malbec, and now it is one of the more popular wines in this country and growing.

Malbec can be quite inky purple in color with black and blue fruit (plum, blackberry, blueberry, and mulberry) and can have some soft violet tones. You will hear wine critics talk about "damson fruit" flavors in this grape. When I was first learning about wine, I had no clue what damson fruit meant. Damson is a type of plum (black skin, black flesh) that is used for many jams and jellies. So when you hear "damson," it is used to describe a plum-like fruit.

Malbec has an incredible affinity for the intense flavors of oak, which means it can have notes of vanilla, coconut, toast, spice, cedar, and/or tobacco. It's fairly soft in its acidity, but that doesn't bother Winters too much. Winters like Malbec for its intense fruit concentration. Its tannins are not as strong as Cab's or Tannat's or Nebbiolo's, but they are dense. Additionally, its alcohol levels can be north of 14 percent, which Winters don't mind at all.

If you are looking for a French Malbec, look for the word "Cahors" on the label. This is the name of one of the best regions in France for Malbec, but the label will not say Malbec. Cahors Malbecs tend to have more raisin and tobacco flavors, while in Argentina they have more lusciously ripe blackberry and blueberry fruit, almost like jam.

PUNTO FINAL MALBEC, MENDOZA, ARGENTINA
Medium deep ruby color, slightly opaque, with some blue tones and with aromas of sweet ripe blueberries, raspberries, plum with slight bramble, toast, and vanilla. On the palate it is rich and dense with balanced acidity, slightly warm alcohol, and tannins that are gripping. Well balanced, and finishes with flavors of blueberries and toast.

PETITE SIRAH (puh-TEET sir-AH)

This little black grape is not to be confused with Syrah/Shiraz (see chapter 9). It is actually completely unrelated. Compared to Syrah/Shiraz, Petite Sirah has a darker color, more dense character, and fruit flavors that are more black fruit (blackberry, boysenberry, plum) and blue fruit (blueberries).

Petite Sirah isn't really "petite" at all in weight. This grape actually makes wines that are "bigger" than Syrah, with a more powerful structure. It may not be as elegant as some Syrah/Shiraz, but Winters will like how wines from Petite Sirah pack a punch. Plus, it can also have some savory aromas that are reminiscent of grilled meat that make it alluring.

Given the grape's powerful structure, you often see oak influence—vanilla, coconut, toast, spice—and the grape can handle it. To me it seems to naturally have a chocolaty or mocha flavor and texture.

California is the best place for Petite Sirah as this grape needs tons of sunshine to ripen, but you can also find wines from this grape in bottles from South America. Given the warmth this grape likes, you will generally get a jam-like character to the fruit.

BOGLE PETITE SIRAH, CALIFORNIA

Deep ruby purple color and slightly opaque with aromas of blackberry jam and mocha. On the palate it has a chocolaty texture with rich concentrated fruit, dense tannins, moderate acidity, and slightly warm alcohol. It has a sweet impression on the palate.

AMARONE (am-uh-ROW-nay)

Amarone—a quintessential Winter wine! Its rich flavor and powerhouse style make this a Winter's dream. Amarone is the name of a wine, or to be more specific, a wine style. It is not the name of the grape. In fact Amarone is made from three different grapes, but you won't see their names on the bottle.

The name Amarone comes from the word for bitter in Italian, "amaro." That is not to say the wine itself is a bitter wine. However, the tannins in Amarone can be quite firm. Its flavor is dense and rich with an element of bitterness, just like dark, bitter chocolate. So, if you said in *The One Minute Wine Master* Quiz that you prefer dark, bitter chocolate, this is the wine for you!

Amarone, unlike most wines, is made from intentionally dried grapes on racks after they are picked. This is an ancient technique in Italy and it results in very rich wine. After the grapes are dried for a few months, the fruit flavor and sugar become more concentrated. Since sugar turns into alcohol through the fermentation process, more sugar yields higher alcohol.

Have you ever made a reduction sauce? The longer you heat and stir a reduction sauce, the more water evaporates, making it more dense and rich. Same principle applies here. Dried grapes make wines that have more concentrated fruit density and higher alcohol than wines made from fresh grapes.

Winters will enjoy Amarone for its dense fruit concentration, chewy tannins, and the warmth of the alcohol. In fact, Amarone can have about 15 to 16 percent alcohol, almost at the level of Port! If you're a Winter and your dinner companion is a Fall, Amarone is a great choice because its dried fruits and spice flavors also appeal to those in that season as well. But a flavor that Winters will truly enjoy is chocolate-covered cherries. This is my benchmark whenever I smell Amarone, and Winters will love these rich flavors.

Amarone comes from the region of Valpolicella in Veneto, Italy, to the northwest of Venice. That's it—only one place. However, don't confuse Amarone della Valpolicella (as it is typically written) with wines labeled only Valpolicella, or another popular wine from that region called Ripasso.

Valpolicella is the red wine of the region with the same name made with fresh grapes, as opposed to Amarone's dried grapes. It is a basic red wine with a soft texture and juicy fruit. While this may sound appetizing to a Summer, it's not powerful enough or rich enough for a Winter.

Ripasso is a bit softer as it is made with wine from fresh grapes "passing over" dried grapes (which is where the name Ripasso comes from). However, given the softer structure and lower alcohol, Ripasso is more of a Fall wine than a Winter one. So Winters, make sure it says "Amarone" on the label.

> *Winters will enjoy Amarone for its dense fruit concentration, chewy tannins, and the warmth of the alcohol.*

MASI COSTASERA AMARONE DELLA VALPOLICELLA, VENETO, ITALY

Medium deep ruby color, slightly opaque with aromas of chocolate-covered cherries, spice, hint of minerals. On the palate it is full-bodied with a chocolaty texture, balanced acidity, dense, firm tannins, and warm alcohol. A well-balanced wine with layers of complexity and a lingering finish of chocolate-covered cherries.

AGLIANICO (al-ee-YON-ee-koh)

This is a dark-skinned grape variety from southern Italy that is so up Winter's alley. Winters will like it for its dark color, black plum fruit flavors, chocolaty texture (and sometimes flavor) and density.

It can also have some smoky flavors, which Winters will also enjoy. It has powerful tannins, which can be slightly bitter to most everyone except those in the Winter category. It also has good, balanced acidity, despite being grown in such warm climates.

This ancient grape variety was brought from Greece by the Phoenicians to southern Italy. You will generally find wines made with Aglianico only under their regional names, such as Aglianico del Vulture, in Basilicata, and Taurasi, in Campania. However you do see more wines with the grape name Aglianico on the label.

MASTROBERARDINO AGLIANICO, CAMPANIA, ITALY
Medium ruby color with aromas of cherry, black cherry, dried herbs, hint of soy sauce and bramble, and minerals. On the palate it is fairly full-bodied with moderate acidity and firm, gripping tannic structure that is slightly drying toward the finish of this moderately complex wine.

TOURIGA NACIONAL
(tour-EE-gah NAS-ee-o-nal)

This fun-to-pronounce grape indigenous to Portugal is one of the grapes used to make Port, that sweet dessert wine we love with chocolate.

It's also used to make dry red table wine. You know all of those mulberry, blackberry, violet, and black-spice flavors you get in Port? They come through in the table wine, too, just without the sweetness that ports have. Winters will like this as well as its powerful structure.

Touriga Nacional can be found in several regions in Portugal, but like so many other European wines, it probably won't say "Touriga Nacional" on the label, though some have smartened up and do now. If you are looking at a bottle of Portuguese wine and you are wondering if it has Touriga Nacional in it, a good tip is to look on the back label. Many Portuguese wineries are now starting to show the percentages of grape varieties. Also look for the region of Douro in Portugal as that is where Touriga Nacional dominates. Winters will love its density, power, and concentrated black fruit flavors, chocolaty texture, and warming finish.

Touriga Nacional is often blended with other grape varieties—other indigenous Portuguese grapes as well as French grape varieties like Syrah and Cabernet Sauvignon. You also see some producers playing with it in Chile, Argentina, California, and South Africa.

QUINTA DOS QUATRO VENTOS, DOURO VALLEY, PORTUGAL
Medium deep ruby with aromas of black fruit, black currant, cassis, licorice, hint of black pepper with notes of vanilla. On the palate it is fairly full-bodied with moderate acidity, good balance, and layers of complex flavors.

MERLOT (mer-LOW)

We mentioned Merlot in chapter 8 as a wine Summers may appreciate. Similar to being born on the cusp of a zodiac sign, cusp wines can flip-flop between seasons. Merlot can be made into soft, plush, juicy wines that could appeal to Summers, spicy wines that will appeal to Falls, or rich, dense, fruity, and powerfully tannic wines that Winters will find thrilling.

> *Merlot is sometimes aged in 100 percent new French oak, which adds a more aggressive structure and flavors of vanilla, spice, tobacco, and cedar. These wines would appeal to Winter.*

It's a black grape variety originally from Bordeaux, France, and is often blended with Cabernet Sauvignon to "beef it up." It is used in Bordeaux to soften and fill in the mid-palate fruit gaps of Cab. It has rich fruit and darker plum character than Cab, but it has nowhere near the tannins that Cab has on its own. So, you may be thinking, why is it in Winter?

In the high-quality Bordeaux regions such as Saint-Émilion and Pomerol, Merlot is a much more powerful grape. Additionally, it is sometimes aged in 100 percent new French oak, which adds a more aggressive structure and flavors of vanilla, spice, tobacco, and cedar. These wines would appeal to Winters.

In California, Washington, and elsewhere in the New World, Merlot is a comfort wine. It has plush black fruit with a soft, supple feel and earthy tones of dried leaves. Some of these may appeal to those in the Fall category.

In northern Italy, there is a region called Trentino where Merlot is grown and generally does not see any barrel age. These Merlots are lighter and more acidic, which would possibly appeal more to a Spring or Summer.

The great thing about Merlot is that, like Cab, you can find it easily and at almost any price.

CHÂTEAU LA BIENFAISANCE, SAINT-ÉMILION, BORDEAUX, FRANCE

Deep, opaque ruby color with aromas of blackberry, plum, minerals, vanilla, and toast. On the palate it is full-bodied with moderate acidity, slightly warm alcohol, and (in its youth) a powerful tannic grip. A very good quality, high-end wine that will age for over ten years.

A NOTE ON BORDEAUX

Bordeaux is usually a blend of Cab and Merlot. It is difficult to know just by looking at the label, however, which wines are made with mostly Cab and which are predominantly Merlot. Ask the sommelier or retail staff, or look for the following words, which are generally good indicators.

Cab-based wines with some Merlot: Saint-Julien, Saint-Estèphe, Pauillac, Margaux, and Graves for the more expensive ones; Médoc, Haut-Médoc, Moulis, and Listrac for more economical values.

Merlot-based wines, perhaps with some Cab or Cabernet Franc: Saint-Émilion, Pomerol for the moderate to luxury end; Entre Deux Mers for more value-priced wines.

ZINFANDEL (ZIN-fan-dell)

We mentioned Zinfandel (aka "Zin") in chapter 9 because it can appeal to Falls. However, this is another cusp variety that can be made in a way that Winters will go gaga over.

We talked about Zin's tendency to be an uneven ripener, which means some of the grapes in the bunch ripen at different times than others. When the winemakers wait for all the grapes to be ripe, some grapes will be a bit shriveled looking, a bit like raisins. Sound similar to a wine we've talked about for Winters? Yep, Amarone!

Zin exhibits some similar characteristics to Amarone, such as a higher concentration of fruit flavors and higher alcohol. I have tasted Zins at over 16.5 percent alcohol! Fruit flavors for Zin range from cranberry and raspberry to black cherry and black currant. It can also taste of dried fruits like raisins and prunes, with black spice and even some smokiness.

Zin can also handle any amount of oak a winemaker throws at it and it won't flinch. Some of the wines that see 100 percent new oak can be quite intense in flavor with a rich, dense chocolaty texture and firm, gripping tannins. Other seasons may have to drink water between sips given its intensity, but not Winters!

RIDGE
CALIFORNIA
LYTTON SPRINGS'

RIDGE ZINFANDEL, LYTTON SPRINGS, DRY CREEK, SONOMA, CALIFORNIA

Deep, slightly opaque ruby purple color with aromas of raspberry, blackberry, smoke, sage, and hint of black pepper with sweet vanilla and coconut notes. On the palate it is full-bodied, warm alcohol with balanced acidity and chewy tannins. Perfect for Winters.

WINTER PREFERENCE SUMMARY	WINTER RESPONSE TO A SOMMELIER:
CONCENTRATION: high	
TANNIN (BITTERNESS AND STRUCTURE): high	"I like my wines full-bodied, intense, and rich with flavor. I prefer powerful wines with strong tannins and I don't mind high alcohol."
ALCOHOL TOLERANCE: high	
ACIDITY PREFERENCE: varies	

ASKING
FOR HELP

"He who is afraid of asking is ashamed of learning."
— DANISH PROVERB

YOU ARE NOW A ONE MINUTE WINE MASTER. You know the styles of wines you like (and possibly wines that your friends will like). So you may be thinking "Why do I need to ask for more help?"

There are literally thousands upon thousands of wine producers and wineries from which to choose. You know you like California Cab? Fantastic! Now choose among the three thousand wineries in California. Like Germany Riesling? Great! Which of its over four thousand villages and vineyard names would you like? What about Burgundy? Fabulous! There are over three thousand producers there.

Each retail shop and each restaurant has its own selection of wineries they like. As I mentioned in chapter 1, some wine stores have more than three thousand wines to choose from. Some restaurants can be worse (or better, depending on your perspective). For example, Bern's Steak House, in Florida, has the largest wine list in the world, claiming they have almost a half million bottles cellared! Though these wines are not all on their wine list, whether you are choosing a wine for yourself or at a client dinner, the choices can be overwhelming. So we can all use a little more help.

I'm a Master of Wine and I generally ask for the assistance of the sommelier. Besides having fun talking shop, I know they taste the wines on their list repeatedly and often. They know how those wines taste "right now" and that is helpful information when making a decision.

WHY DON'T WE ASK FOR HELP?

There are many reasons why people don't ask for help (for that matter, why do men never stop to ask for directions?). Kidding aside, to feel more comfortable asking for wine advice, we first need to bust some myths and eliminate some preconceived notions. We will also look at the type of advice we are getting and from whom.

MYTH #1—THE SOMMELIER IS GOING TO PUSH THE MOST EXPENSIVE BOTTLE.

This is probably our biggest fear when asking a sommelier or retail store person for help. We are scared of being scammed into paying for the most expensive thing on the list (or paying more than what we want).

The Reality: Yes, sommeliers receive a bigger tip if you order a more expensive wine (because tips are a percentage of the bill before taxes). However, this logic is a bit shortsighted. Let's take it one step further:

- » Sommeliers get paid by the restaurant
- » The restaurant wants repeat business
- » Therefore, the sommeliers want your repeat business and they won't get it if you feel cheated

Restaurants and sommeliers want to do everything they can to make you feel comfortable, welcomed, and satisfied. And with more people dining at home these days due to economic pressures, they are working even harder for your business.

To help assuage your fears, when you speak with the sommelier consider saying something like this: "I'm thinking of wines in the $X to $Y price range and I don't want to go above $Y. What would you recommend?"

This way you set the boundaries in advance. If you don't, the sommelier may inadvertently make a recommendation that may be too high or too low. If it's too high and you have to tell the sommelier to go lower (or vice versa), there is risk for both of you to lose face. So establish the range in advance.

That's not to say some sommeliers may not try to up-sell you and push you a little beyond your price range. But, whenever I have had this experience, it was because the sommelier had recently tasted a wine he or she was really excited about. They think it is a great value for the money, they are super passionate about it, and they want to share that experience with you. Remember, any smart sommelier wants you to be pleased and to be a repeat customer. So don't shy away. However, if the wine is clearly out of your range, it is OK to say, "That sounds like a great wine, but for today I'd prefer to stick to wines up to $Y."

MYTH #2—ASKING FOR HELP IS GOING TO MAKE ME LOOK LIKE I DON'T KNOW WHAT I'M TALKING ABOUT.

I think this may also be the reason men never ask for directions. It's the idea that if we ask for help we will look foolish or ignorant.

"It is better to remain silent and be only thought a fool, than to open one's mouth and remove all doubt."

— *Abraham Lincoln*

My father has often repeated this quote to me after I or someone else has said something stupid. While sound advice, I don't believe this is true when it comes to asking questions if you truly want to learn. Being intimidated prevents you from growing, learning, and making better decisions.

The Reality: The only way you learn is by asking questions and asking for help. I didn't become a Master of Wine because I was born with the knowledge. I asked questions. Let me add to that: I asked a lot of questions. I asked sommeliers, retail buyers, winemakers, wine marketers, professors, vine growers, cellar rats, government officials, producers, importers, and distributors. One of the best compliments I ever received was from an ex-boss who said, "There were no questions Jennifer was afraid to ask and her lack of fear is part of why she has seen such success."

You may not have aspirations to become a Master of Wine, but speaking with the sommelier and asking questions will help you look more impressive, not less.

Now that you have completed *The One Minute Wine Master* Quiz (chapter 5) you are armed to speak to the sommelier. You know what you are looking for in a wine and how to communicate it.

For example, if you are a Spring you'll say "I am looking for a light-bodied, delicate, crisp, high-acid white wine." If you are a Winter, you now know to say "I like rich, full-bodied, hearty red wines with a tannic grip." This will go a long way in helping the sommelier narrow the choices and recommend something great, and you will look impressive in the process.

Another fringe benefit of asking the sommelier for help is that you may be offered something "special" not on the wine list. This could be something that just got delivered but isn't printed on the list yet, or something they save for VIP customers.

Years ago (and, I should add, before I met my husband) I was at the Harry Cipriani restaurant in New York City with the famous rock star Bryan

> *Another fringe benefit of asking the sommelier for help is that you may be offered something "special" not on the wine list.*

Adams. (Don't ask how I got there, it's a long story.) On this night, he said to me "Jennifer, choose a *great* bottle of wine." I looked at the list and didn't see anything on there that seemed worthy of a future Rock and Roll Hall of Famer. So I asked the waiter if they had anything special that wasn't on the list. Turned out they had a Barolo that was perfect for what he wanted and for the occasion. I looked like a superstar!

The bottom line is, no one knows the restaurant's wine list or the wines in the store better than the sommelier or buyer. They taste every wine listed and are hoping you will be just as excited as they are about their choices. Why put the entire burden of the choice on your own shoulders? Have them help you out!

MYTH #3—SOMMELIERS ARE CONDESCENDING AND SNOOTY.

We have this preconceived notion that anyone with wine knowledge is snooty. Look at you! Now that you've read this book you have some wine knowledge. Are you suddenly snooty? Of course not!

The Reality: Sommeliers are very passionate about wine. They love talking about wine, love choosing wine, love recommending wine, love tasting wine, and love sharing information about wine. It's their job, their life, their thing! Their number one priority is to serve you something that you will love and that will keep you coming back for more.

Sommeliers also want you to look good to your guests. They are not trying to one-up you or to make you look foolish, especially not at white-tablecloth restaurants. They won't correct you in front of your guests, even if what you are saying is way off base.

Bernard Sun, corporate beverage director for the famous Jean-Georges restaurants, told me a story of just such a situation. One evening two couples

Sommeliers also want you to look good to your guests.

arrived with their own wines. One wine was a white from Bordeaux. As Bernard was pouring the wine for the guests, he heard the gentleman say, "This is a great white Bordeaux. It's made from white Cabernet Sauvignon grapes."

White Bordeaux is made with white grapes called Sémillon and Sauvignon Blanc, not white Cabernet Sauvignon. In fact, there is no such thing as a white Cabernet Sauvignon. But did he correct the guest? No. Was the guest wrong? Absolutely! However, he did not want to make him look foolish in front of his guests.

"These guests came to enjoy themselves with the wines they brought. They did not come for a wine education," says Bernard.

WHAT IS THE PROPER WAY TO ORDER A WINE AT A RESTAURANT?

STEP 1: TAKE CHARGE OF THE WINE LIST

The waiter is going to offer a wine list for the table. If this doesn't happen quickly, then ask for it. I find it is good to get something in everyone's glasses very soon after they are seated, especially when entertaining clients. It puts everyone in a better mood. If someone at the table doesn't grab the list enthusiastically, the waiter or sommelier will just lay it down on the table.

And this is your chance! As I said in chapter 1, most people will shun the wine list or pass it around the table as if in a game of "hot potato." However, this is a golden opportunity to grab the list and shine.

STEP 2: CHOOSE THE WINE

Assess your table's needs, choose a wine, and tell the waiter or sommelier which one you want. Need help choosing wine? See the next chapter for some strategies that will help you make great choices every time.

STEP 3: IS THIS WHAT YOU ORDERED?

The waiter or sommelier will bring your chosen wine to the table and present the bottle with the label facing you. This is so you can make sure it is the bottle you ordered. Sometimes restaurants do not update their wine lists as fast as they should and sometimes the vintage has changed or they may have pulled the wrong wine from the wrong bin. If it is not the wine you ordered, let the waiter or sommelier know immediately, *before* he/she opens the bottle.

STEP 4: OPENING OF THE BOTTLE

The waiter or sommelier will open the bottle tableside, generally next to the person who placed the wine order. Two things happen in this step: the sommelier presents the cork and also pours a tasting sample.

» *Presentation of the cork*: The waiter or sommelier will take out the cork and lay it down on the table. This is not for you to smell or to do anything with. It is simply to show you the condition of the cork. Some people will touch the cork to see if it is still spongy. Cork is a porous material and when the bottle is kept on its side, the wine in contact with the cork keeps it moist and expanded. However, if the bottle is kept upright for too long or kept in conditions that are too warm, the cork can dry and shrink, which can cause seepage and possible spoilage to occur. In other words, it could be a warning sign.

» *Screw cap wines:* Some wines have screw cap closures. Generally in these cases, the sommelier does not present the bottle's screw cap.

» *Pouring a tasting sample*: The waiter or sommelier will pour a small amount (about an ounce) into the glass of the person who ordered the wine.

STEP 5: SAMPLING THE WINE

This is when you smell and taste the sample. The waiter or sommelier has poured for you to see if the wine is in good condition and has no detectable faults. Let me be clear: this is *not* to see if you like the wine or not. It is to see if it is flawed or out of condition. Having said that, if the sommelier really pushed a bottle on you and it was not as described, you may want to say something, and they may or may not take it back. Generally speaking though, you send a wine back only when it is in poor condition or is clearly flawed.

STEP 6: POURING FOR YOUR GUESTS

Once you have given the OK to the waiter or sommelier, he/she will start pouring the wine for your guests. Traditionally, ladies are served first, then gentlemen and the person who ordered the wine last (regardless of gender).

WHEN IS IT APPROPRIATE TO SEND A WINE BACK?

There are several reasons to send a wine back. The two most common are because it is corked or oxidized.

CORKED WINE

This may sound silly given how many wine bottles are sealed with a cork, but when someone says "the wine is corked" they're saying the wine has a flaw.

A "corked" wine smells like an old musty basement. It has a chemical in it called trichloroanisole, or TCA for short. This is the chemical responsible for making your basement smell musty. It's caused by a fungus that metabolizes chlorine to create TCA. TCA in wine can be found in the cork or in the wood at the winery. At best, a corked wine has diminished fruit. At worst, it smells like an old musty basement and is not fit to drink. The smell won't dissipate with time. It won't "blow off." In fact, it will get worse. You need to send it back.

OXIDIZED WINE

Ever cut an apple into wedges and leave it on the counter for a few minutes? What happens? The white flesh of the apple starts to turn brown. That is the process of oxidation. Oxygen impacts wine in a similar way: over time, it can turn the wine brown and can make it taste like sherry or vinegar.

If you order a young wine (meaning the grapes were harvested less than three years ago) and the color is brownish and/or the wine smells a little like sherry or vinegar, then chances are it is oxidized. Again, the wine won't improve with time; you need to send it back.

There are many other wine flaws. For example, when a wine smells like burnt matches or onions or rotten eggs, these are other symptoms of flaws. However, corked and oxidized wines are the main reasons consumers send wine back.

Don't feel intimidated to say to the waiter or sommelier "I think this wine is flawed." That's what you are supposed to do if the wine is in fact flawed. If your waiter is not the sommelier, he/she may call the sommelier over. Don't be scared! They have to inspect all complaints. It could be a problem with that one bottle, an isolated incident, or there is something wrong with the case of wine they purchased.

You should then be given the choice to get another bottle of the same wine, choose a different bottle, or cancel the wine order altogether.

Many people are unsure if a wine is flawed or not. They feel something is wrong but are too embarrassed to send the wine back, worrying that the sommelier is going to challenge them, or they think the wine is just not their style. Don't let this be you! Life is too short to drink flawed wine. The restaurant will bring you another bottle. Promise!

We all need help. Even me! I'm a Master of Wine and I haven't tasted every single wine by every single winery. That would take several lifetimes.

> **Life is too short to drink flawed wine.**

I ask questions all the time. There are many times when I go to a restaurant, I narrow my choices and speak to the sommelier about how these wines are tasting now. Even if I have tasted that wine before, the sommelier has likely tasted it more recently.

Now, if I can ask questions, so can you! That's what sommeliers are there for and they enjoy every second of it.

12

STRATEGIES FOR CHOOSING WINES

I MAGINE YOU ARE IN A RESTAURANT WITH YOUR BOSS and a prospective big client. The waiter drops off a wine list with more than seven hundred wines on it and you are asked to choose one. You want to impress your prospective client (and boss) while not breaking the bank. Your palms start to sweat, you feel the room get smaller, and you are convinced that whatever choice you make the sommelier is going to snicker. I know how you feel. I've been there.

Taking charge of the wine list scares us because we feel the pressure to make the "perfect" choice. But what is the perfect choice?

The reality is, there is no such thing. I understand that saying this may bring you little comfort, but let me explain. Voltaire, the famous French Enlightenment writer and philosopher, said, "The perfect is the enemy of the good." I have found this to be true when choosing wine. Actually, just *making a choice* and being enthusiastic about it, believe it or not, can go a long way toward impressing your boss, client, date, or friends.

However, now that you are your own One Minute Wine Master and you are not afraid to ask for help, it's time to put your new knowledge to use. First, you need to consider your purpose in choosing the wine. From there we can then look at five simple strategies that will help you make the best choice for you and the occasion.

For those of you in a rush who only want the executive Summary of Strategies, go to page 60.

WHAT'S THE PURPOSE OF THE WINE YOU ARE CHOOSING?

So why are you choosing a wine? What's the occasion? Is it to impress a new client or a new boyfriend or girlfriend? Are you just hanging out with friends? Do you need a crowd-pleaser? Is it a gift? Think about why you are getting the wine in the first place.

The reason I ask these questions is that your strategy may vary depending on your objective. For example, if you are buying a holiday gift for a neighbor as a thank-you for watching your kids, your wine-buying strategy can be very different than if you're trying to impress a new client at a fine-dining restaurant.

STRATEGY 1: CHOOSE BASED ON WHAT YOU LIKE AND/OR WHAT YOU ARE PASSIONATE ABOUT

One of the easiest strategies to employ is to base your choice on your own opinion. In other words, choose what you like! Now that you know what your category is and you've tried some of those wines, that should be pretty easy for you.

This strategy is probably the most comfortable one to use because we don't have to think about anyone else, just what we like.

I used this strategy at a business dinner to make a friend of mine look good. At the time I was working for a wine importer and at this dinner were the company's U.S. president and global CEO. I was asked to choose a wine. However, a colleague and friend of mine, Michelle, was also there, and I knew she really wanted to make a good impression.

Making a choice wasn't going to be easy, either. The U.S. CEO looked at me as if to say "Impress the global CEO, but don't spend too much money," and everyone was choosing different entrées, from fish to filet mignon. No one wine was going to fit the bill for everyone. Eeek!

So I chose the wine based on a favorite of Michelle's. I knew she was a Fall and that she liked red wines from the Rhône Valley, in France. When it came out to the table, her face lit up and when she spoke about how she loves Châteauneuf-du-Pape, she positively glowed. She also raved about me (which was an unsought but welcome fringe benefit). Additionally, given that the global CEO of the company was French, he appreciated my choosing a French wine. Unbeknownst to me, it also happened to be one of his favorites. I made my friend look radiant and impressed the CEO. The moral of the story? You can be a superstar by choosing a wine based on someone else's preferences.

When it may not work

Choosing based on someone else's preference definitely works when you are trying to get better connected with your guest(s). If you are trying to shine and the person you are entertaining really, truly doesn't care about the wine choice, however, I might go with my own preferences.

Additionally, if you do not feel confident in what you like and you don't want to press the issue with your guest(s), then I would suggest getting a recommendation.

STRATEGY 3: ASK THE SOMMELIER TO CHOOSE

What happens when you are at a restaurant, you look at the list, and nothing looks familiar and your guests seem just as flummoxed? This is when you need to get a recommendation from the sommelier.

As discussed in chapter 11, sommeliers are there to help you. It's their job to help make the best choice for your event. They also have an inherent interest in keeping you happy; they want you to come back.

Benefits of this strategy

One major benefit of this strategy is that it takes the pressure off you and your guests. If nobody likes the choice, it's not your fault! The sommelier or wine waiter has chosen and tasted all the wines on the list; this should help you feel confident that you are in good hands.

This is also a great strategy to use if you have narrowed your choices to, say, three wines on the list and they all look so good you can't decide. The sommelier or wine waiter will have tasted the wines and will know which one is tasting the best right now.

However, you do have to help the sommelier out a little by letting him or her know some parameters such as price, what you are eating, and some of your preferences. Now that you've gone through *The One Minute Wine Master* Quiz, identifying these preferences will be a bit easier.

When this doesn't work

Actually, this strategy almost always works really well, with two exceptions: if you don't communicate what you really want to the sommelier, or if the sommelier is not very good. Most of the mismatched recommendations I see, however, are the result of bad communication to the sommelier. So please make sure you are clear by using the summaries in your category and offering examples of wines you think could be appropriate (even if they are not on the list). Try to describe as specifically as possible what you are looking for.

However, if you do choose this strategy, there is one thing you should never do: *Never* haggle with the sommelier.

While I was working for a wine importer, I met a friend (who shall remain nameless) at a trendy new restaurant in midtown Manhattan. I had been there quite a few times, but this was my first visit with this friend.

This friend has been known to be quite finicky about food and wine, so I narrowed the choices to three and decided to speak with the sommelier. However, my friend interrupted to ask, "Is there something on this list that you personally picked out that is not selling but is an amazing value that no one knows about?"

I thought this was a great question! However, after the sommelier responded, my friend then asked, "What will you give it to us for? Obviously we don't want to pay full price. Since it's not selling, you should give us a deal."

Though the sommelier was polite in saying they don't haggle on wine prices, I was completely embarrassed. I also got a call from my boss the next day saying the restaurant complained to my company (I had no idea they recognized me) and politely asked that I never visit their restaurant again.

STRATEGY 4: CHOOSE BASED ON BUDGET RANGE

This is a very easy strategy to use if you are not confident about your choices or the knowledge or the preferences of your party. You can use this strategy when all you know is how much you are willing to spend.

Most people, not wanting to appear cheap, won't choose the least expensive wine on the list. And at the top of the list, people are scared of breaking the bank. So, most of us try to choose something in the middle.

The most important thing, however, is to actually have a dollar figure or price range in mind. If you go to a restaurant with no idea how much you're willing to spend on a wine you may be setting yourself up for buyer's remorse, feeling cheated, or for unrealistic expectations on how the wine will taste.

So do yourself a favor: have a sense of what you want to spend before you open the wine list. It should be a range you can easily communicate to the sommelier or wine waiter. Remember, they want you to come back.

Benefits of this strategy

Basing your choice on budget protects your wallet. To make the best use of this strategy, let's take a look at where the values are on a wine list.

Restaurants charge more for the same bottle than a retail store does. While a retail store may mark up a bottle of wine by 25 to 30 percent over its cost, it is common for a restaurant to double or triple its cost to arrive at the selling price. Some wines are made in such tiny quantities that sheer economics of supply and demand drive the price up.

Generally speaking, wines at the least expensive end of the spectrum have the highest markup. This can be three (and I've seen five) times the price you would see at a retail store.

Likewise, those at the most expensive end of the spectrum also have a high margin. On a per-bottle basis, these represent huge profits for the restaurant. However, there is less volume at the high end. It's not every night that an average restaurant will sell a bottle worth over $1,000.

So where are the good values on a wine list? A good rule of thumb is to take the average price of an entrée and multiply by three. That should be where the lowest margin, and therefore better values, are. For example, if the average cost of an entrée is $20, then your best values will likely be around $60. However, this is a huge generalization (as rules of thumb usually are) and may not be applicable everywhere. But it's a good place to start.

When this doesn't work

The only time this strategy doesn't work is when you have no idea what you want to spend or you are choosing based on someone else's budgetary consideration. This is easy to address—just think about it in advance or talk it over with the person with the wallet. The only other time this strategy doesn't work is when money is no object. May we all have that problem someday!

STRATEGY 5: CHOOSE BASED ON WHAT PEOPLE ARE EATING

A "magic" food and wine pairing can change someone's life. No joke! A food and wine pairing changed my life forever (see the Introduction).

But food and wine pairing is not easy. Even in the trade, most people don't know what a "good" pairing is, let alone the intricacies of creating "great" pairings. That's why you see such old saws as "red wine with red meat" and "white wine with fish." Though huge, sweeping generalizations, they can be true and help give people a starting point.

Using food pairing as a strategy to choose wine is fantastic when dining at a restaurant with a specific focus, assuming everyone is willing to go along. So let's say you are going to a steak house. Chances are that a red wine will pair with the filets mignons and rib-eye steaks that everyone is ordering. If you are at a seafood restaurant and everyone is ordering fish in some form (poached, broiled, fried, etc.), a crisp white wine is a fairly safe bet. Another good idea is to order a wine that matches the geographic origin of the food. So, if you are in an Italian restaurant, it makes sense to order an Italian wine.

The major wrench in this system is that everyone won't order the same thing, even if that restaurant has a particular theme. Mom orders the sautéed sole, your husband orders the rib-eye steak, and your brother has the fettuccini alfredo with chicken. So now what?

One option is to go with one of the other three strategies listed above and to hell with how well it pairs with the food. The problem with that, though, is that it can be a missed opportunity for food-and-wine-pairing bliss.

Also, many people have no idea what "pairing well" means. I've written a cookbook with a Certified Master Chef named Ken Arnone. Among the over six hundred food and wine pairing trials, one great pairing was a Sancerre (Sauvignon Blanc) with grilled scallops. Sancerre is made with 100 percent Sauvignon Blanc, which has fresh, crisp acidity (see chapter 7). The wine's high acidity cuts through some of the richness of the scallop, making the dish seem refreshing and light, and the grilled marks actually brings out the wine's complex mineral tones. The sweetness of the scallops also brings out the wine's citrus and floral notes.

However, sometimes it easier to see a good pairing when you have a bad pairing to compare to. If you tried the same dish (grilled scallops) with a rich, full-bodied, buttery, heavily oaked California Chardonnay, the wine would totally overpower the scallops. This means that you would taste only the wine;

the flavor of the dish would be covered up by the wine. Even if you are a Fall, and you love these wines and don't mind that it is covering up the dish, understand it is not a good food and wine pairing. The best are two-way pairings, meaning when the dish improves the wine and the wine improves the dish (such as the Sancerre and grilled scallops).

If everyone is choosing different entrées, pick something very middle of the road from the Summer or Fall category. Many times in those scenarios I have gone with California Pinot Noir as it is more in the Summer category, with plush fruit that will almost satisfy the steak eaters and without harsh tannin for the fish eater. You have to be careful, though; a chemical reactions occurs between some wine and fish where you taste a strong metallic flavor (e.g., sea bass with Pinot Noir).

This would be another good time to ask the sommelier for help. Not only do the sommeliers or wine waiters know the wines, they have likely tasted all the dishes as well.

FAMILY AND FRIEND RECOMMENDATIONS

In *The One Minute Wine Master* I am attempting to give you recommendations based on your own palate, not my personal preferences. However, it can be quite fun to speak with and get recommendations from friends and family on wines they like.

After all, they know you personally. This strategy works when the person knows quite a bit about wine or if they know what you like and can steer you down the right path.

The risk is that their suggestions will be based on their personal preferences and palate, and they may or may not be the same as your own. For example, you could be a Spring and your friend a Winter. Unless your friend has your particular palate in mind, it will be almost impossible to suggest a wine you will like.

However, this is easy to test! Just take a minute and have them do *The One Minute Wine Master* Quiz (chapter 5) to see if their category or quiz responses are similar to yours.

WINE RATINGS

Just as the movie industry has critics, so does the wine industry. However, instead of thumbs up and thumbs down, wines are usually given ratings. These ratings can be in the form of symbols (such as stars or wine glasses) or numbers (such as 18 out of 20 or 88 out of 100).

Relevance of a wine critic's ratings is one of the most hotly debated topics in wine. Why? For some of the same reasons that family and friends aren't always the best source of recommendations. Wine critics' knowledge is also called into question and whether they can look past their own personal preferences to give an unbiased critique.

I have heard many sommeliers and wine buyers scoff at ratings. I think there are three main reasons: (1) sommelier job justification, (2) sommeliers trust their own palate more, and (3) sommeliers have a philosophical objection to putting a number on a topic that is so complex.

Regardless of anyone's feelings about ratings, they are here to stay. This is especially true now that a new wine blogger seems to pop up every day. Sommeliers and store buyers have to pay attention to ratings because many consumers base their buying decisions on them; when a 95 out of 100 point rating comes out, some sommeliers will be the first to buy, regardless of their philosophical beliefs. They're in business, after all.

Many critics specialize in a particular area, and my theory is that they choose it because it fits their palate's preferences. I'm not saying critics are unable to look past personal preference. All I'm saying is that personal preference is hard to ignore and does come through in their writing.

For example, Jim Laube of *Wine Spectator* magazine is well known in the industry for rating highly red wines that are very bold, tannic, and concentrated. Based on how he writes his reviews and the high scores he gives to high-octane wines, I might guess he's a Winter. If that were true, and you are a Winter, then great! You would know a critic who suits your palate. His recommendations could lead you toward wines that would suit your palate.

Another example, perhaps at the opposite end of the spectrum, is Jancis Robinson, a British Master of Wine who has made a huge contribution to the industry.

I trust her palate immensely, in part because she is a fellow MW. She was tested and given an international title for being able to analyze wine and to look past her own personal preferences. However, she does indicate in some of her writings that she loves wines that have finesse and crisp acidity and that offer refreshment. Though I haven't quizzed her, based on her writings, I can guess her preferences might suggest she is the perfect critic to follow if you are a Spring.

The important thing to keep in mind is to follow critics who suit your palate. It takes time to develop trust in the recommendations of a critic, but once you do, this strategy can work very well.

GIFTS

Wine makes a great present, especially for those people you have no idea what to give or for corporate gifts. Many firms have an under-$50 gift policy, and a bottle of wine can be a great way to say thank you.

Most of the strategies we've discussed so far are for a consumption environment, typically at a restaurant. However, you can use the same concepts when buying gifts at a wine store or online. Some tips to keep in mind with gifts:

» If you are going to choose based on your own preferences, let the gift recipient know how passionate you are about the wine. This will make the gift more personal and they will think of you when they open it.

» Many people purchase recognized brand names to make sure the recipient is aware of the care taken to choose the gift. This can work to your advantage or disadvantage depending on the recipient's palate and/or thoughts on the specific brand.

» Put the wine in a box or special wrapping. I recommend doing this on your own as some wine stores' wrapping can actually work against your gift. With just a little effort you can make a $15 wine look like a $50 package and make a great impression. My mom always told me, "An ounce of image is worth a pound of performance."

SUMMARY OF STRATEGIES

STRATEGY	BENEFITS	WHEN IT WORKS	WHEN IT DOESN'T WORK
Choose wines you like	• Conversation starter • You sound more confident • Passion is infectious	• You are very passionate about specific wines you like • Trying to impress clients, new boy-girlfriend, boss, friends. This is when you want to shine and talk about something that you are passionate about.	• The boss/client wants to choose the wine • Your choice goes against the theme of the group, restaurant, or event (i.e., Spring wine among all Winters) • You are not confident in your preferences
Choose wines your guests like	• Takes some of the pressure off of you • You appear quite gracious • Make the boss/client look good • Conversation starter	• You are not confident in your preferences • The boss/client wants to choose (or shine)	• You want to take charge and impress • You really know what you want

(continued next page)

STRATEGY	BENEFITS	WHEN IT WORKS	WHEN IT DOESN'T WORK
Ask the sommelier to choose	• Takes all the pressure off • You are in good hands • You can blend this strategy with others	• You are not confident in your or your guests' choices • You've narrowed your choices to a few wines and can't decide	When you haven't really communicated what you want to the sommelier
Choose based on budget	• Protects your wallet • You can blend this strategy with others	• You are not confident in your or your guests' choices • You can't decide between a few favorites	When you don't know what you want to spend
Choose based on food pairing	• Can be used with other strategies • Can make "magic" happen	• When everyone orders the same type of cuisine/ entrée • Order based on a theme	Everyone is choosing different items and no one wine will fit the bill
Choose based on recom- mendations (friends, family, ratings)	Takes the pressure off	Recommender knows a lot about wine and what you like	Recommender has opposite palate to you and recommends only what he/ she likes

FREQUENTLY ASKED QUESTIONS

HOW DO I OPEN A BOTTLE OF WINE THAT IS SEALED WITH A CORK?

Step 1—Cut off the foil (you can either use the small knife that is on the corkscrew or you can buy a separate foil cutter).

Step 2—Wipe off any dust or anything else that might have collected on top of the cork.

Step 3—Place the tip of the corkscrew spiral in the middle of the cork.

Step 4—With a gentle twisting motion, press and twist the spiral into the cork so that it stays in the middle of the cork as you screw down. Do this until the entire spiral is in the cork.

Step 5—Use the lever on the side of the corkscrew for leverage and gently pull the cork almost entirely out of the bottle, but not quite. Some corkscrews have only one lever; those with two make it even easier.

Step 6—Place your hand around the cork and pull it out the rest of
the way. If you pull the cork out too fast and too hard with
the corkscrew, there can be spillage. I've done this many
times, so be careful.

WHAT'S THE BEST TEMPERATURE FOR WINE?

The usual advice is that whites should be chilled and reds served at room
temperature. This is not bad advice, but it's not entirely accurate, either,
since people have different definitions of "chilled" and "room temperature."

The average refrigerator temperature is about 35–38°F (2–3°C). This is a
bit too cold for white wines. Chilling makes wine seem fresher on your palate,
but if it's too cold the aromas and flavors will be completely muted. Serve it too
warm and the fruity aromas decrease and the alcohol will stand out, making
the wine seem unbalanced.

Here is a rough guideline using *The One Minute Wine Master* categories:

Spring and Summer whites	44–48°F (7–9°C)
Fall whites	48–52°F (9–11°C)
Spring and Summer reds	52–55°F (11–13°C)
Fall and Winter reds	55–59°F (13–15°C)

Average room temperature in a restaurant or in your home is likely to
be anywhere from 70 to 75°F (21 to 24°C). Many of us at home, and
sorry to say at many bars, keep the reds on the counter and they warm
up to room temperature. Served at 70–75°F (21–24°C) the wines change,
and not for the better. Luxury restaurants with outstanding wine service
generally serve reds in the 55–60°F (11–16°C) range and don't serve reds
over 65°F.

I suspect the advice to serve reds at room temperature came from northern

Europe. It may just be me, but every time I've traveled there, their room temperatures are much colder than they are here in the United States. I think this is why they layer clothing with shirts, light sweater, jacket, and scarves. Their room temperature is below 65°F (18°C)!

Do you have to get a thermometer before you drink a glass of wine or buy a wine storage unit that keeps all your wines at exactly the right temperature like they do at some luxury restaurants? No, there's a perfectly good low-tech (and low-cost) way of doing this. Put whites in the refrigerator and when you are ready to drink them let them warm up a little (and wait a bit longer for the heavier Fall whites). I might put Spring and Summer reds in the refrigerator a little while before you are ready to open them so they chill down a bit (but don't leave the bottle in for too long or you will have to wait for it to warm up). I would keep Fall and Winter reds in a cool dark place (i.e., *not* on top of the refrigerator or next to the oven on the countertop).

HOW LONG CAN I KEEP AN OPEN BOTTLE BEFORE IT GOES BAD?

That depends. Some say up to three days, but I've seen people keep an open bottle in their refrigerator for months. I find that wines taste different the next day. In fact, I've often asked for a fresh bottle if the wine by the glass at a restaurant tastes like it has been open for too long. But if you don't notice anything amiss, don't worry about it.

To keep your wines after they've been opened, put them in the refrigerator (yes, even reds). This will slow down the process that eventually would turn the wine to vinegar.

> *I find that wines taste different the next day.*

However, there are ways to keep them even longer, such as using inert gas. Private Preserve is an aerosol bottle of inert gas that you spray inside an open bottle of wine. The inert gas is heavier than air, so oxygen is pushed out and the inert gas lies on top of the wine like a blanket. This further slows down oxidation and the development of acetobacter (the bacteria responsible for turning wine into vinegar). This can help keep wine drinkable for as long as a week or so. There are also wine vacuum sealers such as Vacu Vin, though I find them less effective than inert gas. But they're better than just sticking the bottle in the refrigerator with the cork.

As a last resort, you can always cook with the wine that is left over. Another option is to immediately freeze leftover wine in ice cube trays and keep it for when you make sangria!

WHAT TEMPERATURE SHOULD I STORE MY WINE?

If you are keeping wine only for the short term (under a year) or medium term (a few years) just make sure that you keep your wine in a dark, cool place where there isn't too much temperature fluctuation.

Without doubt, one of the worst places to store your wine is above the refrigerator. Heat rises and it can get pretty warm up there—the wine can literally cook. Just don't do it!

The ideal temperature for storing wine for long-term aging (beyond a few years) is 55°F (12.8°C) at about 60 percent humidity. The temperature should be fairly constant and it should also be dark, as ultraviolet light can accelerate wine spoilage.

HOW LONG CAN I STORE WINE (UNOPENED)?

I would say that 90 percent of all wine (maybe more) is intended to be consumed within three years of its vintage date. For example, if the date on the bottle is 2012, then it is probably made to be consumed by 2015 (particularly for white wine). Though not an official benchmark, I do think it is fairly safe to say that the majority of wines under $25 are best from three to five years old. Only a small percentage of wines can last and age longer than that, and even fewer will improve with age.

I HEAR THAT IF YOU LET A WINE "BREATHE" IT TASTES BETTER. IS THAT TRUE?

Letting a wine "breathe" refers to the act of exposing the wine to air (or, more specifically, to oxygen). The reason for this is that the wine's reaction to oxygen allows more aromas to develop and be released. Some wines can taste dramatically different after they've been allowed to breathe.

Though most wines will open up with a little air, letting a wine sit and breathe (especially longer than an hour) will not necessarily improve it. Generally speaking, decanting and breathing for a few hours is reserved for more expensive wines, particularly those that have the structure to age.

However, some people think that letting a wine breathe means opening the bottle and letting it sit on the table upright for hours. The amount of wine exposed to oxygen that way is the size of a quarter, so not much reaction is going on. Pouring the wine in a decanter, however, circulates lots of air through the wine and is much more effective.

Every wine is different, so there is no hard and fast rule to tell you how long to let wines breathe (especially wines from older vintages). Older wines have a shorter window of peak drinking after being opened and allowed to breathe. So there is a risk of missing some of the best flavors if you leave an old bottle decanted and let it breathe for hours.

> *Every wine is different, so there is no hard and fast rule to tell you how long to let wines breathe.*

WHAT'S THE DEAL WITH VINTAGES? DO THEY REALLY MATTER?

The beautifully mysterious thing about wine is that weather patterns in a particular year impact a wine's color, aroma, flavor, structure, and how long it will last. However, before you start memorizing vintages, understand that vintages are not equally important in every wine region. For example, Burgundy and Germany are cool climates and they vary more widely in their weather patterns than warm climates (such as Napa Valley).

Knowing vintages is imperative when investing in expensive wines, and wines you intend to lay down for longer than three to five years. You can also save money by recognizing a good deal on a vintage when you see it.

If you want some ideas on great vintages and how long to age wines you may want to look at vintage charts. Below are great sites that have vintage charts:

> » *Decanter* magazine: www.decanter.com
> » *Wine Report* by Tom Stevenson
> » *Wine Spectator*: www.winespectator.com
> » *Wine Advocate:* www.erobertparker.com

DO ALL WINES GET BETTER WITH AGE?

When I first met my husband the only thing he knew about wine was the phrase "the older the better." Unfortunately, this is not true for all wines. As I mentioned, only a small percentage of wines improve with age. But what does "improve with age" mean?

Many people have no idea what "improved with age" means or tastes like. Does a wine that has improved with age taste just as it does when its young (fresh and fruity), but just "better"? How? I must confess I had these questions when I first started.

The first wine I had with some age on it was in 1999. It was a 1976 Château Latour, a first-growth Bordeaux whose cost at the restaurant was more than the cost of my first year of college (needless to say, I was a guest and was not picking up the tab).

Before this I had really tasted only young, fruity California wines and I expected to see a rich, deeply colored wine with even more dense, jammy fruitiness; that's what I thought "better" meant. I was way off in this respect, but delighted in another.

As red wines age, they lose their color (become paler and move toward orange or tawny), and become leaner in body (moving from heavy cream toward whole milk) and less tannic. White wines gain in color (go toward gold and tawny colors) and can increase in weight. Additionally, a wine's elements—flavor, texture, acid, alcohol, and tannin—become more seamless, and you hardly notice where one begins and another ends. A wine's fruitiness also goes down while other Fall-like flavors are more pronounced (for example, spices, earth, leather).

The structure of the 1976 Latour was seamless and harmonious; it was more complex than anything I had ever tasted before. So many layers of flavor, and those flavors lasted for such a long time, continuing to give new sensations and nuances as I savored each sip. Though it didn't taste the way I expected, it was far better than what I thought "better" meant.

My point in telling you this is for you to understand what happens to a wine when it ages and to have a realistic expectation of what it will taste like. If you do not like the flavors, textures, or profile of an aged wine, then don't age your wines for more than a few years.

I know people who love the fruitiness of young wines so much they won't drink anything more than five years old while others won't touch wines unless they are at least two decades old.

> *If you do not like the flavors, textures, or profile of an aged wine, then don't age your wines for more than a few years.*

HOW MUCH DO I TIP FOR WINE IN A RESTAURANT?

Tipping 15 to 20 percent before tax is customary for good to great service. Anything above 20 percent suggests excellent service and below 15 percent is considered fair to poor. This is with the wine included on the bill.

But what if you bring your own wine? If you want to share something special with guests at a restaurant, many restaurants will allow you to bring your own wine—for a fee. They will charge you something called a corkage fee.

Do yourself a favor and call the restaurant in advance to find out what the corkage fee is, so that you are not surprised. I've seen corkage fees from $10 to well over $100 per bottle. Safe to say, it doesn't make sense to bring a $15 bottle if you are going to be charged $25 corkage.

If you do bring your own wine, your tip will vary depending on the restaurant, the wine you bring, and their corkage fee. Some say to tip 20 percent of what the bottle would have cost on their list or tip the price of the corkage fee, whichever is higher.

Each situation is different, so you will have to use your best judgment. Know, though, that it would not be fair if you brought in a $100 bottle and you tipped only $4 (20 percent of the $20 corkage fee), especially if the restaurant provided excellent service. That's just not cool.

WHY DO I GET A HEADACHE FROM SOME WINES?

There is no one answer to this question as there are several possible culprits—sulfites, histamines, dehydration, and of course drinking too much. Understand, too, that people's reactions to wine vary widely according to their health, their gender, and genetics.

> *People's reactions to wine vary widely according to their health, their gender, and genetics.*

Pretty much all wines have sulfites, though some do not have "added sulfites" and some claim to have no sulfites. In the United States, wines with more than 10 milligrams per liter are required by law to state "contains sulfites" on the label, and wines are not allowed to have more than 350 milligrams per liter.

People who are allergic to sulfites will have a reaction to sulfites in wine. If you think sulfites are the culprit of your headaches from wine, try this test. Eat some orange-colored dried apricots. Some of them can contain sulfites as high as 2,000 mg/kg (*way* more than any wine you will ever try). If you don't have a reaction, your headache is not caused by the sulfites in wine.

Many people complain of headaches with red wines. This can be due to the histamines they contain. Histamines are found in the skins of grapes, and as the juice sits on the skins (to get that color), they seep into the wine.

Have you ever taken an antihistamine when you have allergies or a cold? Antihistamines suppress your body's reaction to histamines, which cause your sinuses and head to feel stuffy and achy. To be clear, I am not suggesting you blend antihistamines and red wine; I'm simply trying to demonstrate how histamines impact your body.

The alcohol in wine also dehydrates your body. Depending on how much wine you drink, this can cause headaches as well as all the awful feelings of a hangover the next day. This is why it is a good idea to drink water when you are drinking wine. Some suggest drinking one glass of water for every glass of wine, but this will vary from person to person (and with the size of the glass).

Some people have said they get headaches only with Champagne or sparkling wine. This could be a result of drinking too much of it (as bubblies are usually consumed at celebrations) or because the carbon dioxide (those bubbles) make the alcohol run through your system faster, getting you drunk faster and dehydrating you faster.

ANY IDEAS FOR A WINE-THEMED PARTY?

What better way to taste many different kinds of wines with your friends than having a wine-themed party? Here are a few suggestions:

» *The One Minute Wine Master* party—Invite your friends and pick some wines from the various categories, have them take the quick quiz, and walk around and taste. Arrange a room with a table in each corner to represent each of the four seasons. You will have something for everyone, and your guests will have a blast tasting and talking about the wines.

» *Wine and cheese party*—Pick a theme, such as Spanish wines with Spanish cheeses or French wines with French cheeses or American wines with American cheeses. It can be fun to alternate different countries (and a good excuse to continue to get together).

» *Wine blending party*—Play winemaker! Ask people to bring various wines made with 100 percent of a particular grape variety (Cabernet Sauvignon or Merlot or Malbec or whatever) and have your guests make their own blends and see which ones they like. It's like finger painting, but for adults!

» *New wine party*—Invite guests to bring a wine they themselves have never had before (perhaps use *The One Minute Wine Master* Wheel as a guide). This can help you try new wines you never would have considered before.

These are just a few ideas to get you started. Wine-themed parties can be so much fun!

One theme that I would save for later in your wine journey is a blind wine party, where guests bring bottles covered with aluminum foil or brown paper bags in order to render them unidentifiable to the other guests. Everyone then tastes, analyzes, and tries to guess the wines' identities. The reason I can't recommend this theme at early stages of learning is because someone will invariably feel uncomfortable with guessing and afraid of looking foolish in front of others. So unless your friends are genuinely as excited as you are to do this, I'd skip it for now.

I WANT TO LEARN MORE ABOUT WINE. CAN YOU RECOMMEND ANY BOOKS OR MATERIALS?

There are too many great wine resources to list, but here are a few that will provide more in-depth information about the vast world of wine:

» *Encyclopedia of Grapes* by Oz Clarke
» *The World Atlas of Wine* by Hugh Johnson and Jancis Robinson, MW
» *Wine for Dummies* by Ed McCarthy and Mary Ewing-Mulligan, MW
» *The Oxford Companion to Wine* by Jancis Robinson, MW
» *The Everyday Guide to Wine* by The Great Courses (24-episode DVD series, with yours truly)
» *The Sotheby's Wine Encyclopedia* by Tom Stevenson
» *Wine Report* by Tom Stevenson
» *Windows on the World Complete Wine Course* by Kevin Zraly (this was my first wine book and it is fabulous and gets better with every new edition!)

THREE ADDITIONAL QUIZZES

THE ONE MINUTE WINE MASTER QUIZ

QUESTION	3 POINTS	
1. How do you take your coffee or tea?	Black/nothing added	
2. How much sugar do you add to your coffee or tea?	None	
3. What type of chocolate do you prefer?	Dark, bitter chocolate	
4. How often do you put lemon on your fish?	Never	
5. What is your favorite juice?	Apple	
6. How spicy do you like your food?	Extremely hot	
7. If you compare the body of a white wine to the body of heavy cream, whole milk, or skim milk, which would you prefer?	Heavy cream	
8. If you compare the body of a red wine to the body of heavy cream, whole milk, or skim milk, which would you prefer?	Heavy cream	
9. What type of perfume or cologne do you like?	Spicy/intense	
10. What type of gum do you prefer?	Spicy (cinnamon)	
11. What is your favorite snack?	Something rich like chocolate or a candy bar	

KEY

SPRING: 1–13 POINTS
SUMMER: 14–19 POINTS
FALL: 20–25 POINTS
WINTER: 26–33 POINTS

2 POINTS	1 POINT	0 POINTS	TALLY POINTS
A little milk or cream	A lot of milk or cream	I don't drink coffee or tea	
A teaspoon	Two or more teaspoons	I don't drink coffee or tea	
Milk chocolate	White Chocolate	I don't eat or like chocolate	
Sometimes	Always	I don't eat fish	
Orange	Lemonade	I don't drink juice	
Medium	Mild	None	
Whole milk	Skim milk		
Whole milk	Skim milk		
Sweet/candied	Floral/fresh	I don't like perfume or cologne	
Bubble gum or fruity gum	Fresh (mint, violet, etc.)	I don't chew gum	
Something savory like chips or crackers	Something light like a piece of fruit or carrot sticks	None of these	

TOTAL POINTS

THE ONE MINUTE WINE MASTER QUIZ

QUESTION	3 POINTS	
1. How do you take your coffee or tea?	Black/nothing added	
2. How much sugar do you add to your coffee or tea?	None	
3. What type of chocolate do you prefer?	Dark, bitter chocolate	
4. How often do you put lemon on your fish?	Never	
5. What is your favorite juice?	Apple	
6. How spicy do you like your food?	Extremely hot	
7. If you compare the body of a white wine to the body of heavy cream, whole milk, or skim milk, which would you prefer?	Heavy cream	
8. If you compare the body of a red wine to the body of heavy cream, whole milk, or skim milk, which would you prefer?	Heavy cream	
9. What type of perfume or cologne do you like?	Spicy/intense	
10. What type of gum do you prefer?	Spicy (cinnamon)	
11. What is your favorite snack?	Something rich like chocolate or a candy bar	

K
E
Y

SPRING: 1–13 POINTS
SUMMER: 14–19 POINTS
FALL: 20–25 POINTS
WINTER: 26–33 POINTS

2 POINTS	1 POINT	0 POINTS	TALLY POINTS
A little milk or cream	A lot of milk or cream	I don't drink coffee or tea	
A teaspoon	Two or more teaspoons	I don't drink coffee or tea	
Milk chocolate	White Chocolate	I don't eat or like chocolate	
Sometimes	Always	I don't eat fish	
Orange	Lemonade	I don't drink juice	
Medium	Mild	None	
Whole milk	Skim milk		
Whole milk	Skim milk		
Sweet/candied	Floral/fresh	I don't like perfume or cologne	
Bubble gum or fruity gum	Fresh (mint, violet, etc.)	I don't chew gum	
Something savory like chips or crackers	Something light like a piece of fruit or carrot sticks	None of these	

TOTAL POINTS

THE ONE MINUTE WINE MASTER QUIZ

QUESTION	3 POINTS
1. How do you take your coffee or tea?	Black/nothing added
2. How much sugar do you add to your coffee or tea?	None
3. What type of chocolate do you prefer?	Dark, bitter chocolate
4. How often do you put lemon on your fish?	Never
5. What is your favorite juice?	Apple
6. How spicy do you like your food?	Extremely hot
7. If you compare the body of a white wine to the body of heavy cream, whole milk, or skim milk, which would you prefer?	Heavy cream
8. If you compare the body of a red wine to the body of heavy cream, whole milk, or skim milk, which would you prefer?	Heavy cream
9. What type of perfume or cologne do you like?	Spicy/intense
10. What type of gum do you prefer?	Spicy (cinnamon)
11. What is your favorite snack?	Something rich like chocolate or a candy bar

**K
E
Y**

SPRING: 1–13 POINTS
SUMMER: 14–19 POINTS
FALL: 20–25 POINTS
WINTER: 26–33 POINTS

2 POINTS	1 POINT	0 POINTS	TALLY POINTS
A little milk or cream	A lot of milk or cream	I don't drink coffee or tea	
A teaspoon	Two or more teaspoons	I don't drink coffee or tea	
Milk chocolate	White Chocolate	I don't eat or like chocolate	
Sometimes	Always	I don't eat fish	
Orange	Lemonade	I don't drink juice	
Medium	Mild	None	
Whole milk	Skim milk		
Whole milk	Skim milk		
Sweet/candied	Floral/fresh	I don't like perfume or cologne	
Bubble gum or fruity gum	Fresh (mint, violet, etc.)	I don't chew gum	
Something savory like chips or crackers	Something light like a piece of fruit or carrot sticks	None of these	

TOTAL POINTS

ACKNOWLEDGMENTS

Many have provided inspiration and motivation in the creation of this book.

I thank my darling husband, Christopher, for his unconditional love, devotion, friendship, and support. Everyone should be as blessed as I am to have such an incredibly supportive and loving husband. This book would not have been possible without his passion for the idea (and me).

I also thank my family for their love, support, and enthusiasm. My mother, Michelle, has a gift. If she can taste a dish she can make it with no recipe and it was her love of food and taste sensations that started me on my path in the first place. I thank my father for instilling in me an unwavering discipline and focus. I aspire to his level of integrity and honor in all things. Additionally, I thank my sisters, Elizabeth and Katherine, for their creativity, inspiration, and the ability to always lift my spirits.

I also thank my grandparents. My grandfather, Joseph, began a successful writing career in his seventies and inspired me to write this book. My grandmother, Caroline, taught me to never give up. I also thank my grandfather, Felix, who always said that I "can-do" and to my grandmother, Arlene, for reminding me to always have a little fun.

I also thank Kevin Zraly. Like many of his students of the Windows on the World Wine Course, I was ignited by his energy and passion for wine. His encouragement, kindness, and support have helped me get to where I am today.

And to the countless friends, peers, and colleagues who have influenced and supported me, I thank you.